P9-CAT-828

Mark-making

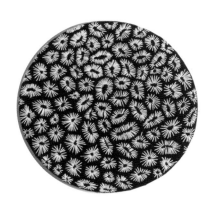

Helen Parrott

Mark Making

Fresh Inspiration for
Quilt and Fiber Artists

INTERWEAVE
interweave.com

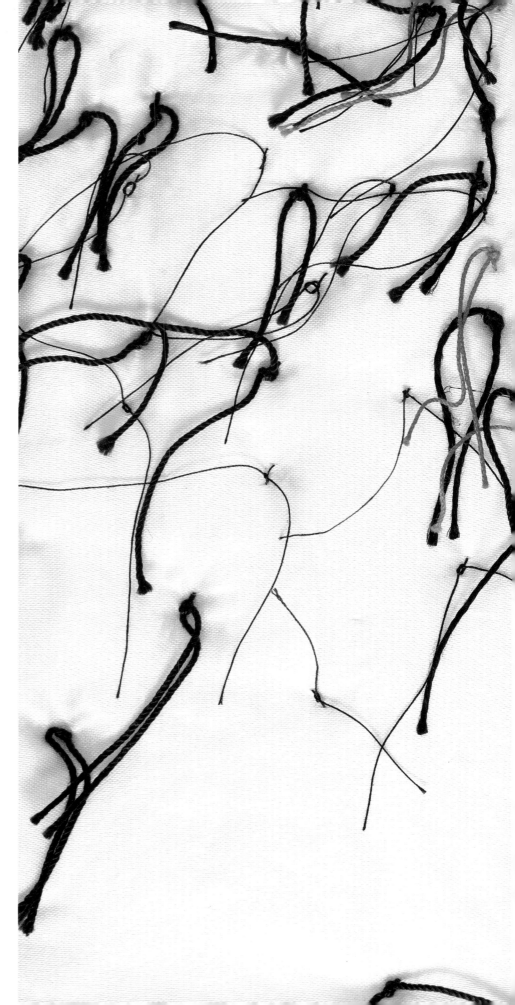

First published in the United States in
2012 by

Interweave Press LLC
A division of F+W Media, Inc
201 East Fourth Street
Loveland, CO 80537
interweave.com

Copyright © 2013 Batsford
Text © 2013 Helen Parrott

The moral rights of the author have been
asserted.

All rights reserved. No part of this
publication may be reproduced, stored
in a retrieval system, or transmitted in
any form or by any means, mechanical,
photocopying, recording or otherwise,
without the prior permission of the
copyright owner.

ISBN 978-1-59668-879-7

Reproduction by Rival Colour Ltd, UK
Printed and bound by Craft Print
International Ltd, Singapore

Page 1: *Harmonious Living.*
Coralline stich, white on black.
Page 2: *Cup and Ring I* (detail). Machine-stitched
marks with applied machine-wrapped cords.

Right: Sample. Knotted stitch
marks made with different types
and thicknesses of thread.

Contents

1 Introduction

If you have picked up this book, the chances are that you are intrigued by the possibility of, or are making, your own textile artwork. You may already have seen and admired the work of other textile artists and makers and want to make your textile work more individual. You may be starting out on your creative journey through a formal course, or you may be an experienced artist seeking fresh ideas. The creation of textile artwork has enriched my life and journey: in this book I hope to share some of this richness with you, to support and facilitate your creative life.

The subject of this book is the making of stitched marks. Many textile arts have traditionally been about stitch. Hand stitching, in its many distinct local and historical forms, has been used across the world for centuries, stretching back into prehistory. More recently, sewing machines have added the possibility of machine-stitched marks to the creative process. Hand stitching and machine stitching each produce very different marks; they can be used separately and together. The book explores some of this vast mark-making potential with a focus on personal expression and creativity.

Stitched work can be seen on items of clothing, bedcovers and wall hangings held in museums and in other public and private collections. Historical stitched textile work was often functional rather than personally expressive, but at their best, historical pieces often exhibit beauty and utility in exquisite textiles made for status and for show. However, humbler, more ordinary stitched textiles that have survived the passage of time often have their own particular beauty and social significance. I remain very drawn to, and inspired by, the traditional hand-stitched wholecloth bed quilts from northern England made in the nineteenth and early twentieth centuries. These bed quilts were for domestic use and have a subtle beauty as well a specific historic, social and economic context. Examples are shown on pages 22, 94, 106, and 125.

Today, many of us are able to choose to work with textiles in a way that is less concerned with the functional and utilitarian purposes of keeping warm or expressing wealth and status. We often make our textile pieces for personal use and for our own creative satisfaction. I feel that the quest for beauty and creative self-expression continues to be important and a fundamental part of what it is to be human.

Right: *Red Circle,* approximately 6½ft x 6½ft (2m x 2m). Knotted stitch marks made with different types and thicknesses of thread.

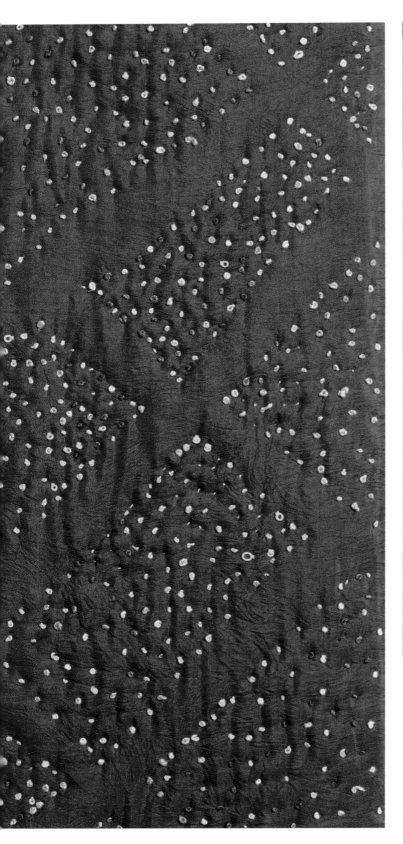

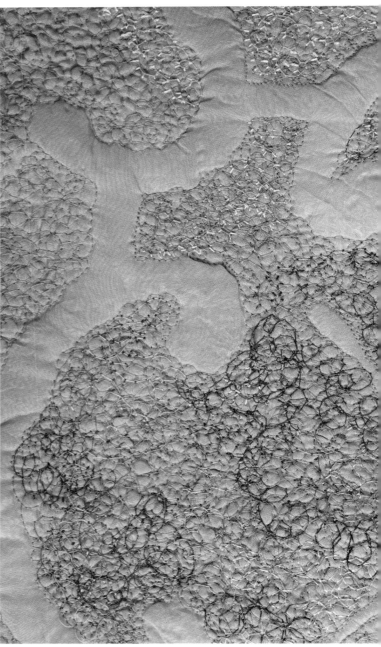

Left: *Field Path
(Buttercups)*. Detail
showing crossed
shapes and knot marks.

Above: Knot garden
machine-stitched
sample (detail).

Using this book

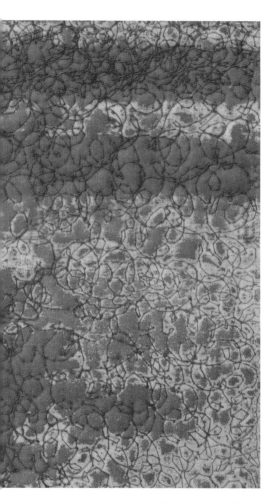

Red machine-stitched marks with red paint.

The intention of this book is to inspire you to begin or, more likely, to continue, your personal creative textile journey. It is intended to be a practical and useful guide to support and sustain you, and not to be kept in pristine condition on a shelf—rather, it should be more of a well-thumbed guidebook.

Of course, as with most guidebooks, this one is both biased and personal. It covers the journey from inspiration and ideas to making marks on paper and in stitch; from reflecting and selecting what to develop to completing textile artworks. Photographs recording my inspirations and interests are included, together with paper works, diagrams and samples that reveal the journey to a completed work. There are suggestions for further exploration, drawn from activities that my students have enjoyed and found useful over the years. Some of them are based on using words alongside visual materials, to inform and clarify your interests and approach. There are also practical strategies, including how to manage your time. Some of these explorations, suggestions and strategies will resonate with you and some will not; others may be useful to you in the future.

I have included some case studies as a way of sharing the choices, processes and decisions involved in making. My intention is to illuminate a creative process, not to provide any kind of blueprint for success.

There has been a recent expansion in the availability of materials and techniques for artists and makers, opening up many exciting new possibilities. However, these choices can seem overwhelming, especially if you are new to making your own personal stitched textile work. This book will enable you to find and to strengthen your personal creative voice.

I seek to share my pleasure in the processes of making art textiles as well in the finished pieces. There are sections on keeping your work moving, materials and equipment, suppliers, some further reading and a list of useful organizations.

A personal view

I have been on my creative journey since the late 1980s, when I was recovering from a period of illness. I began making things for my home and then went to art college to do a course in embroidery. The making of personally expressive art textiles was fundamental to the recovery of my health. I have taught and exhibited in the UK, and further afield, ever since.

My original training as a geographer and my other interests and sources beyond textiles and the visual arts are important to me in exploring, understanding, and expressing what I want to say about living here and now. This book is about ideas arising from my life, experiences, and places (you will have your own to draw on), and the textiles that resulted.

I firmly believe that the most satisfying creative work is distinctively one's own. Such work develops over time, encouraged by regular practice and reflection, interaction with supportive people, and engagement with the world. The work of others can inspire us deeply, challenge and inform us; however, ultimately, we each have our own creative life to live and our own textile artworks to make.

Opposite: *Cup and Ring I*. Detail shown above.

Right: Circles in the snow in a local garden.

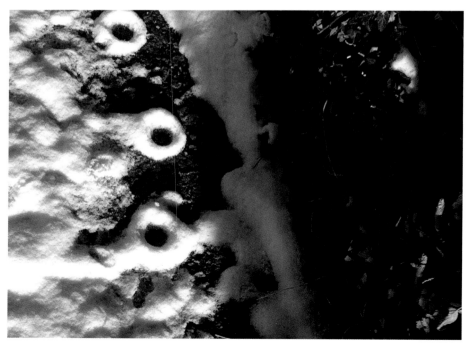

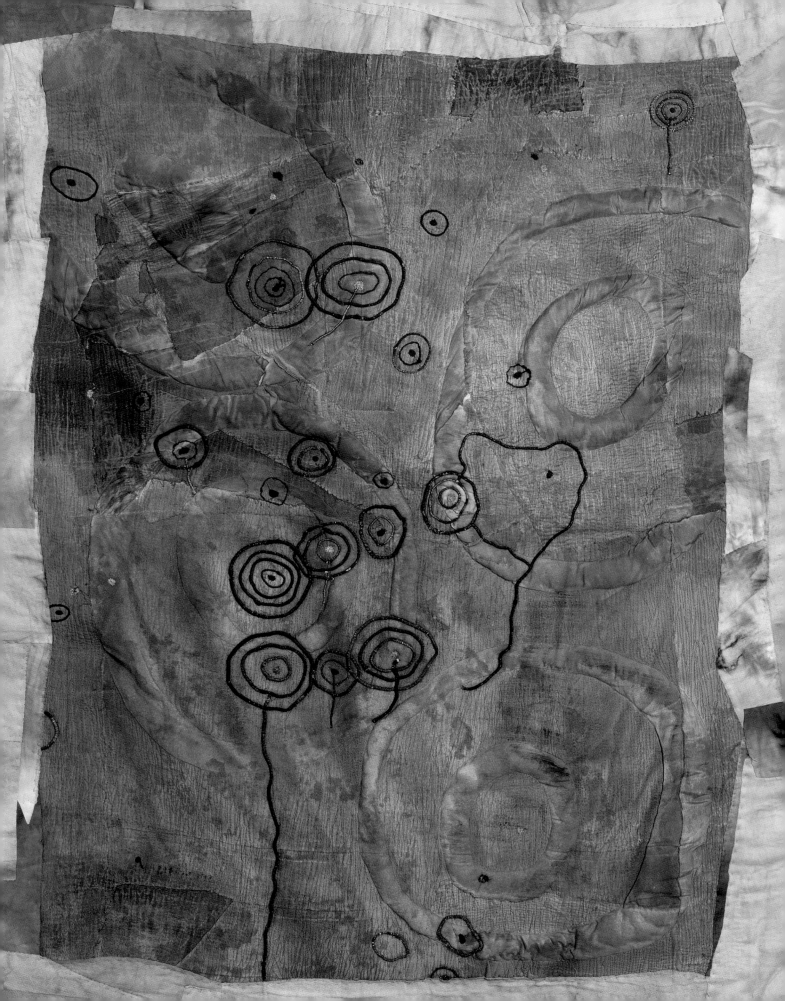

2 About marks

Introducing marks

Marks surround us. They are fundamental to our lives and our learning. Children may be deeply and happily occupied in making marks with crayons on paper or other less suitable surfaces. Handwriting remains a powerful and personal form of mark-making. We still sign important documents, such as contracts, by hand, to make them legally binding. We use the expression 'making a mark' to describe the attainment of recognition or distinction. Marks can indicate ownership of objects and places. There is something powerful in making marks, wherever they occur in our lives.

Look hard at the marks around you and then consider which could be used in your personal textile work. For example, on a walk I may see condensation trails from airplanes marking the sky, the furrows of a ploughed field marking the earth, tree branches against the sky, or the scattered patterns of wild flowers marking a meadow. Once you start to notice marks, you will find that they are everywhere and many are worth exploring as a basis for making stitched textiles. Look for marks in ceramics, sculpture, photography, painting, architecture, and gardens. The world of science, too, is one of many other potential sources of visual inspiration.

Below: Condensation trails in the sky; roadside debris after heavy rain; trees.

Opposite: *Shifting Sands VII,* 24in x 34in (62cm x 87cm).

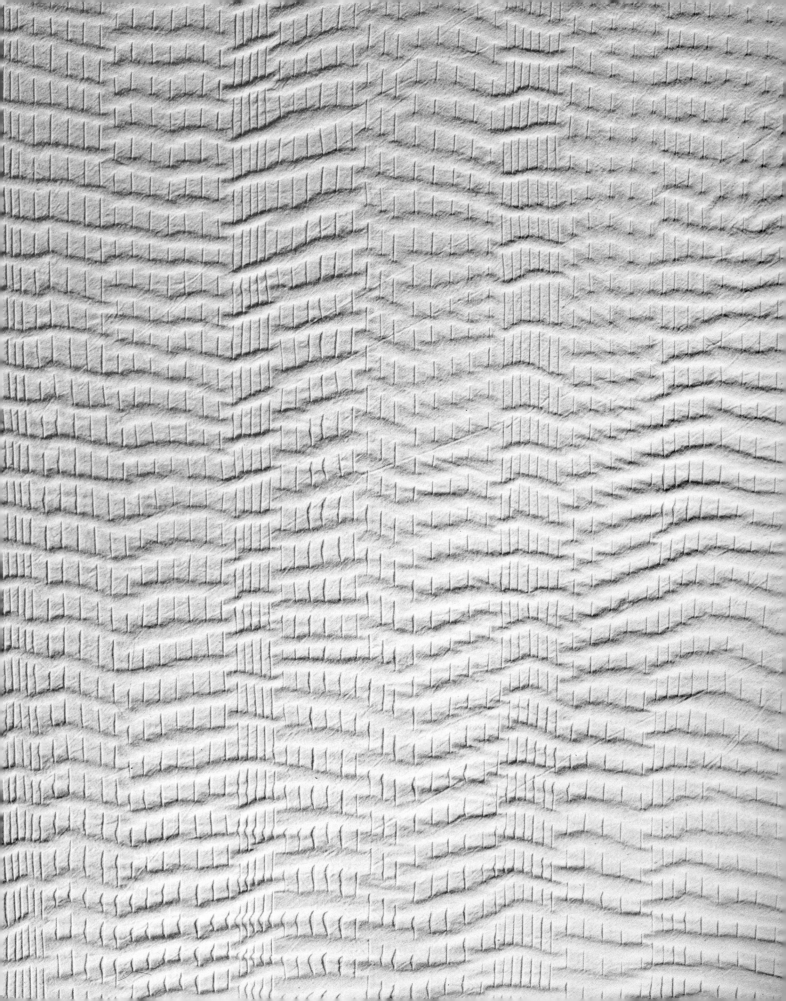

A regular journey can be an especially rich source of marks. It is often traveled at different times of the day and throughout the seasons of the year. The regular traveler can look repeatedly at the marks en route, noting their forms and colors, considering their stability or their transience, and mulling over their potential creative applications. For example, on my railway commuting journey I observe extensive fields of oilseed rape as the seeds are sown, grow into plants, flower, and then the seed crop ripens. Each stage brings different colors and shapes to the fore; each offers some potential for the further exploration of marks.

When you see an interesting mark, record it in some way for safekeeping and then explore and develop it further at your leisure. You may already have an existing working vocabulary of marks that inspire you: this chapter aims to encourage you to broaden the range you use through a richer observation of marks around you, exploring new marks as well as potentially deepening your use of old favorites.

Working with repeated marks

We often think that life is shaped by our relationships, family, education and career. Whilst this is certainly true to a considerable extent, it is also the simple actions of everyday living that do much to create the texture and quality of our individual lives. My long-standing interest in using repeated stitched marks reflects the important role of small, ordinary, repeated actions in life. For example, in *Surface Interventions* on page 77, looped stitch marks are repeated across the surface of the textile.

On a very different scale, it is the repeated actions of the weather, tides, and seasons that have created and continue to create the physical landscape we live in. The grains of sand on a beach have so much more meaning when they are considered as part of the larger picture of geological and other landscape processes.

Left, top to bottom: Field tracks seen from Monsal walking trail, Derbyshire; boat repair, Tarbert, Hebrides; cup and ring-marked stone, Ilkley Moor; fishing net, Filey; reed beds, Humber estuary.

Opposite, left to right: Hawthorn branches, Derbyshire; road sign, St Ives, Cornwall; barbed wire bundle, Abney, Derbyshire.

Considering marks

Marks are often quite complex. They can occur alone, be repeated, juxtaposed, or mixed and overlaid in a myriad of ways. They can be seasonal or permanent, momentary or enduring, artificial or natural. They can be celebratory or aspirational. As you practise observing marks in nature, their potential for creative exploration and use as a basis for making stitched textiles should become clearer. The photographs on pages 14–18 show a range of marks.

Sometimes the potential of such images as a basis for stitched work is very clear. Of the images shown, the fishing nets, barbed wire and reed beds could translate directly into stitched marks using both hand stitch and machine stitch. The harbor handrails shown on page 16 show bold and exciting marks, yet their creative stitch applications are probably less obvious. All these images are part of my collection and may lead one day to completed textile artworks.

Characteristics of marks

As can be seen in the photographs on pages 14–18, marks may have a variety of individual characteristics, such as shape, scale, color, form, direction, origin, or purpose; their relationship to time, their number, density, and location or position may also be significant. The possible combinations of these characteristics are infinite, of course. Consider the headings below as you seek out and assess marks for potential use in textile work.

Shape

What shape is each mark? Is it a circle, square, triangle, dot, dash, line, hexagon, arrow, or star? Is it perfectly shaped or irregular? Are the marks separate or are they continuous in some way, like a dotted line or grid?

Scale

Marks occur on a range of scales, from those that are microscopic to those that are the size of a continent. Scientific images are a fascinating source of marks at various scales, for example highly magnified photographs of tiny cells and pollen grains, satellite images of vast mountain ranges, and fractal patterns derived from computer models, repeating the same mark or shape at different scales.

Color

What color or colors are present? Are the marks monochrome? Are they present as solid or shaded areas? Do the colors vary in some way or remain exactly the same?

Form

Are the marks flat or raised? Are they shaped in some way? Is there a texture? Is the whole surface textured, or only part of it?

Direction

Are the marks positioned in one direction, or in many directions? Is there a central focus, or do the marks cover the whole surface evenly with no direction? Do the marks radiate from one, or several points? Are the marks in rings like a sawn cross-section of a tree trunk? Are the marks present as lines of movement like footprints in sand?

Origin

How were the marks created? Were they made naturally, such as tracks left by birds or animals, or were they carved by people? Were they machine-made or fabricated? Were they created by wind or water, or by using a tool of some kind such as a brush or stick?

Above, clockwise from top left: Stencilled numbers, Humber riverside; detail of a lobster pot, St Ives, Cornwall; floral temple offerings, Singapore; harbor railings, Hebrides; window, Wortley Top Forge, South Yorkshire; riverside plants, Thames Valley, Oxfordshire; carved granite cross, St Ives, Cornwall; detail of stacked deckchairs, Filey.

Opposite, left to right: Poppies, Flamborough, Yorkshire; old roadside kerbing, Houndkirk, Yorkshire; desert plant, Alice Springs, Australia.

Purpose

Many marks have, or had, a purpose. Sometimes the purpose is not known to us, for example when we look at ancient rock carvings or cave paintings. Some marks have a clear purpose: to communicate precise messages to specific people using methods such as Morse code, Ordnance Survey map symbols and semaphore. In public buildings, signage shows visitors where to enter and how to move through the building. Roads are lined with signs to give both directions and warnings. Alternatively, consider more indirect signage, such as the barbed wire that blocks access to a field.

Relationship to time

Most marks have some relationship to time. It is worth thinking about this relationship as it may provide an insight into why a mark is of interest to you, and this may then inform the development of your work. Time may be relevant in several ways: in the time needed to create the marks, in their enduring nature, or in their seasonality or transience. Long shadows cast by the setting sun change from moment to moment, estuarine sand ripples change with every tide, and gritstone seen in a seaside cliff may have taken millions of years of geological time to be created.

Number

Is there one solitary mark or are there many? Are the marks thinly scattered or densely made?

Position/location

Where are the marks located? Are they patterned all over the surface or a part (or parts) of it? Are they parallel or convergent? Divergent? What about the spaces between them? Are they layered in some way? If so, how many layers are there and how are they positioned?

Working with marks and words

Above left: Painted and rusted metal joint, Tarbert harbor, Hebrides.

Above right: Peeling paint, Humber riverside.

Opposite: 'Marks can Be'. Word list for describing marks.

Making art textiles is a visual and tactile experience in many important ways. However, it can be useful to use words alongside these aspects to inform and clarify your interests and approach. The explorations in this chapter all use words in various ways. Do keep the words you write and the notes you make safely: you may wish to add to them later, or revisit them at some future point.

Exploration 1: The marks you use at present

Find a quiet space and time to think about the marks you use (or would like to use) in making textiles. Then look at your photographs, notes, sketchbooks, and personal textile work. Consider what you see. Are there marks and patterns that you are strongly attracted to, or that you use frequently? Do you use one type of mark a great deal? What are the characteristics of the marks that appeal to you? How do you create the marks? What techniques do you use? Do you use hand or machine stitching? Do you draw with pencil, charcoal, or paint? Use print or dye?

Make some written notes to describe what you notice about your chosen marks and the mark-making techniques you like and use. Keep reflecting on what you see, making notes until you have nothing more to add.

Exploration 2: Describing specific marks

Find a set of marks that appeals to you, perhaps from a folder of images or postcards you have kept for future use, or from a favorite illustrated book. Look at the marks you have chosen and start to describe them in words. While this may seem an unfamiliar approach for working in a visual medium, it is often very helpful to analyze marks in your own words. It can sometimes be a challenge to

thin
painterly
thick

pierced

lacy
lively
foliate
arched
directional
striped

checked

additive
subtractive
positive
negative
erratic
dotted
dashed
symbolic

smooth

rough
intentional
tidal
tracks
sequential

personal
hand-written
drawn
painted
printed

sprayed

etched
stitched
quilted
embroidered
anonymous
directive
faint
fading

bold

zigzag
wavy
punched
pinked
scalloped
rough
pierced
undulating
solid
uneven

jagged

forked
curved

looped

continuous
all over
colored
delicate

crisp

sharp
fuzzy
porous
bumpy
temporary
angled
raised
parallel

spontaneous

hand-made
vertical
horizontal
grid
complex
patterns
rings
central

Surface Interventions (detail of loop stitch). Black linen thread on calico layers. The full piece is shown on page 77.

find exactly the right word for an aspect of a mark that appeals to you, and it is a satisfying moment when you find the right description. The more precisely you can describe your chosen marks in words, the clearer and stronger you are likely to be when adapting and using the marks in your textile work.

For example, the difference between the description of a mark as 'jagged' or as 'erratic' could be vital in deciding how to develop the inspiration. You may choose very different equipment and methods as you move forward. Pinking shears make a jagged and regular mark, but not one usually described as erratic. Seeking to make an erratic mark on your work is likely to require a different technique and equipment.

There are some starting points for describing marks in the word list 'Marks Can Be,' shown on page 19. For additional descriptive words, do refer to a thesaurus or dictionary.

When I applied the guidelines of 'Exploration 2: Describing Specific Marks' to some of my digital photographs of road and pavement markings (see opposite), the results were informative in developing my ideas further. My first choice of words was: 'colorful,' 'transient,' 'hand-sprayed,' 'irregular,' and 'calligraphic.' When I repeated the exploration, my second set of words was: 'directive,' 'contemporary,' 'urban,' 'related to a specific location in London that I like and visit often,' 'evocative,' 'good memories.'

Exploration 3: What do other people see?

When you have completed the previous exploration of describing specific marks at least once working alone, find some suitable volunteers. Show them the images of your chosen marks and ask them to describe to you what they see.

When I showed my volunteers the road and pavement mark images shown left and below, their answers were often very different to mine. Their answers included the practical observation that the marks were for locating services below the ground, so blue must mean water and that they had seen similar marks in other English cities recently. The use of these answers could lead to the development of textile work in a quite different direction from that of my own ideas—my initial abstract and color-based thoughts could lead to artworks exploring the colors or hand-sprayed nature of the marks. Alternatively, the association of the marks with enjoyable memories of visits to London and other places could be explored, with very different results.

You may also find that there is little or no match between your descriptive words and those chosen by others, and no consensus on the meanings of images and marks. This is where the voice of the individual maker, his or her reflections, selections, and decisions during the creative process come into play. No two people would make the same art from the same inspiration, which is part of what makes creativity so fascinating.

Above: Pavement marking, London.

Below: Road and pavement markings in London and Scarborough.

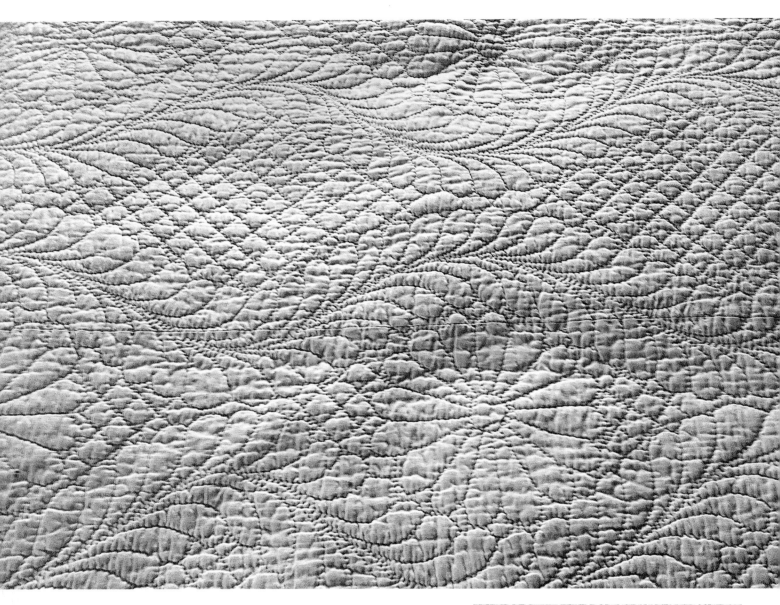

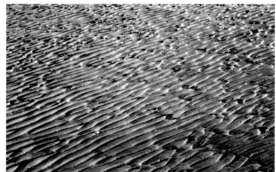

Recurrent words

Exploration 4: Finding your recurrent words

Extend the previous exploration by describing several other marks and techniques you are drawn to or use regularly. Your list of words is likely to be distinctive and unlike anyone else's list. Do any specific words stand out or similar words recur in the descriptions of each mark? You may enjoy choosing one or two of the recurrent words to focus on and explore more deeply over a defined period.

If no individual words are repeated in your lists or there are no groups of closely related words, it could be that your interest lies in a wide range of marks, and by recognizing this you can find a new direction for your textile work.

Working with recurrent words can provide new directions and ideas and enable you to strengthen the distinctive aspects of your work. For example, the images shown opposite and on pages 27, 64, 94, and 125 give a sense of the inspiration for a body of work, with the recurrent words 'hand-stitched,' 'irregular marks,' 'broken lines,' 'subtle,' 'unique,' 'minimalist,' and 'wholecloth.'

The resulting works were made using long, hand-stitched marks, placed in roughly parallel lines, worked freely (not marked on the fabric before stitching), and set on pale-colored, layered wholecloth (borderless) surfaces. *Room to Roam* (see page 25) shows one of the smaller pieces from this series.

Left: Section of North Country wholecloth quilt showing hand-stitched traditional feather, flower, and grid designs.

Below left: Estuarine sand ripples, Wells-next-the-Sea, Norfolk.

Below: Winter snow road, Cumbria.

More about marks

Variability

Hand-made stitched or drawn marks usually have a pleasing variability and irregularity that is not generally found in machine-made marks and the smooth-surfaced finishes of many manufactured objects. Variability is often an attractive quality in textiles and drawings, giving a sense of the person who made the piece through seeing the marks he or she has made, and we often enjoy having a sense of the hand of the maker. Subtle variability is also found in the natural world. For example, no two leaves, pebbles, or seashells are exactly the same. We often associate nature and the hand-made with beauty. Personally, I find that this subtle variability is often part of what I consider to be beautiful.

Placement

We have already noted that marks have many characteristics, including their position and location. The placement of marks is important in expressing an idea. A single mark may be placed centrally or off-center, as a repeat pattern of some kind, in a definite line or track, or as numerous all-over marks. Marks may also be layered or combined. It is worth considering whether the specific placement of marks suits the overall idea being developed. For example, the placing of the lines of hand-stitched marks in *Red Radiant* (see page 107), radiating outwards from a central focus, was key to the idea for the piece. Placing the marks in a different layout, in parallel lines for instance, would not have expressed the idea as strongly as the radiating layout did.

Texture

Marks can create texture. Texture is an important aspect of working in textiles, particularly in layered or quilted work. Think of the texture of carved stone details on buildings or sculpture, for example. A slightly raised or flattened mark, or area of marks, can significantly or subtly change the look of a piece of textile work.

We have now explored many of the aspects of marks in some detail. I hope the potential of marks as the basis for work in stitch is becoming clearer to you. Now that you have begun to look at marks as more complex entities than you may have previously, it is time to move on to finding and creating your own marks.

Opposite: *Room to Roam,* 16½in x 11½in (42cm x 29 cm).

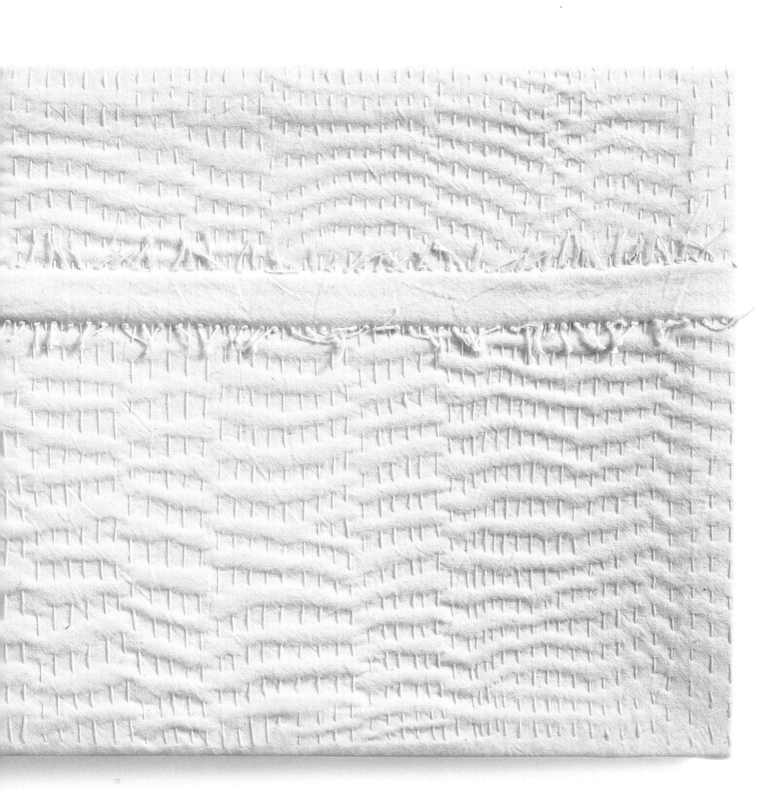

3 Observing, recording, and collecting marks

We are surrounded by marks in our daily lives. By working through the explorations in the last chapter, you will hopefully have clarified your understanding of marks and discovered which marks appeal to you and why. This chapter explores the recording of marks using photography and drawing. The collection of marks is key to achieving more individual and distinctive design work and stitched textiles.

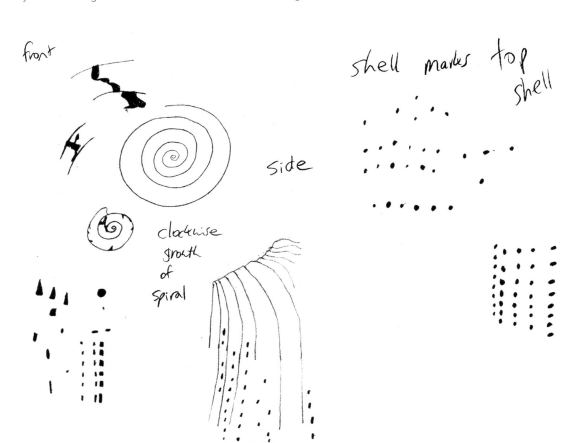

Right: Initial pen and pencil sketches and notes based on shells in my collection.

Opposite: Fossil ammonite found in Whitby and limpet shells found in the Hebrides.

Developing awareness

We all have a personal and distinctive visual view of the world. Life presents us with many, many things to see: some are very interesting, others less so. We often glance at things in passing rather than studying them thoroughly. When thinking and talking about making, I use the word 'observing' to mean a slower, quieter, and more focused type of looking—selecting what may be potentially interesting from the plethora of changing visual information around us. You can then decide which items are worth the time and effort of recording. By becoming more observant, you will clarify your personal visual interests, and this is important in developing your textile work.

The importance of a record

In our daily lives we see a great deal and generally recall very little of it, so it is important to make a physical record. Capture interesting marks before they disappear from view (or the light changes) by making a brief drawing or note in your sketchbook (if you happen to have one with you), or by taking a photograph with your phone or camera. Record the marks in a way that makes clear what attracted you to them. Add written notes to ensure that you have enough information for any subsequent creative work. Any record you make needs to enable you to recall what you observed and why it appealed to you, nothing more! Over time, you will build a powerful resource for future textile work.

Springtime walk

For example, while walking in the woods taking photographs to record the arrival of spring in the valley, I observed an interesting scarred tree trunk. The light was good, so I took several different photographs of the tree and its context. Once at home, I printed the photograph that attracted me most strongly—the scar left where a branch had broken off—and stuck it into my sketchbook. Then I added brief written notes on the characteristics of the scar (see left). Later, I reviewed the image and my notes and added further thoughts (see page 51) on the image and why it had attracted me.

Whiteley Woods Spring 2012 — tree scar
Scar — history — breakage
tension — stretching — compression — expansion
rounded triangle
lines like string — echo shape

Left: Sketchbook page: tree scar image and associated words.

Photograph of tree trunk with
scar of a broken branch, seen
in early spring in Whiteley
Woods, Sheffield.

Observing marks

Exploration 5: Looking at the world around you

Start by examining the world around you at home, preferably in good daylight, first at a normal scale and then at a larger scale with the use of a magnifying glass. Natural objects such as shells, stones, feathers, corals, seed heads, flowers, plants, and so on are fascinating. Some examples are shown below and right.

Choose an object and look at it from all angles, holding it up to the light and examining it thoroughly—this can sometimes reveal previously invisible details and marks. Such marks can have a surprising depth and complexity. For example, when held up to the light, the small Scottish limpet shells shown on page 27 revealed a checkered pattern of growth lines, almost like a Scottish tartan. (This grid of lines occurs where the inner and outer growth lines on a shell cross, and is only visible in a good light.) It can be helpful to think of this process of looking as an exploration of the essential character of an object as shown by the marks on its various surfaces.

What characteristics do the marks have? Look only at the marks, not their colors or the overall form of the object you have chosen. Leaving aside the distractions (and seductions) of color and shape helps to focus the mind. The careful examination of an object to find all the marks it displays can be a very useful exercise for developing stitch marks. There are often exciting and surprising marks to be found on apparently familiar objects.

Below: Natural objects collected over time and used as inspiration for paper works and stitch marks. Clockwise from top left: coral pieces, chalk pebble, pink crystal structure and seed heads.

Opposite: Explorations 5 and 6—pen and pencil sketches based on Scottish limpet shells with some notes on how the marks could be developed in stitch.

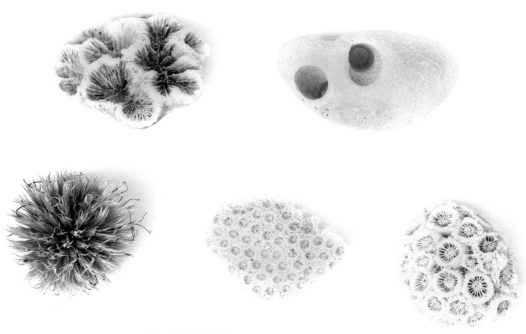

shell marks - limpets

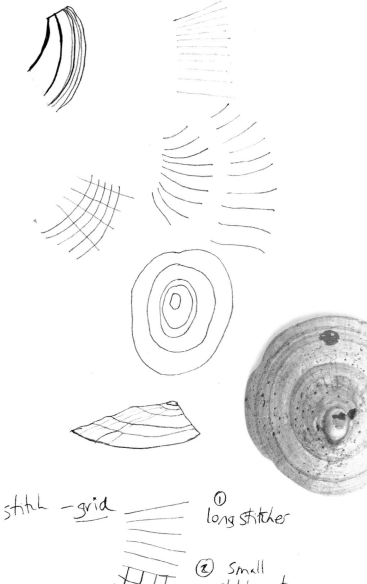

B B limpet
    scallop
    Topshell
B B cone

∘ deeper grooves
between coloured
bands than
within them

∘ fine almost
translucent radiating
lines flaring to
edge

∘ **grids** show
through translucent
shell layers

∘ notched edges

∘ pearly interior

∘ beige/cream/
white/khaki/
green/charcoal/
navy -subtle

⊙ loop couched down
varied threads
? larger as
oval enlarges

stitch - grid

① long stitches

② small
stitches to
hold long ones
+ make a grid

Ochre pits, West
MacDonnell National
Park, Northern Territory,
Australia, showing the
rock structure.

Recording marks

Exploration 6: Recording what you observe

When you have studied your chosen object thoroughly and inspected it with a magnifying glass, record all the marks you see by making a sketch. Your aim is simply to record the marks, not to create an accurate drawing or illustration. This practice is about capturing the energy and range of marks you see in a way that will remind you of what you observed.

The sketches shown on page 26 and 31 are initial records of the marks observed on two shells in my collection. I prefer to use pencils and felt-tip pens, usually working with black, gray, or dark brown to ensure that I focus on the marks themselves rather than their colors. You may find that other art media are more suitable, depending on the range of marks you wish to capture (see page 39 in the next chapter).

Most of the quick sketches illustrated offer some starting points for mark-making, design work, and creating stitch marks. Some may have sufficient potential for a complete textile artwork, although it can be quite hard to tell at this early stage.

As previously mentioned, written notes can be useful for providing information for later creative development. I often add notes on the colors seen, as I find it distracting to try and record color using paints or crayons at this stage. Words are more direct and evocative for me.

Taking photographs

The idea of making sketches can be a challenge for some people. The knowledge that a sketch is a record made for personal use only and not intended as a finished article is not always sufficiently reassuring. However, the ready availability of cameras in mobile phones has made it easier than ever before to record things of visual interest, whenever and wherever you are. Indeed, sometimes a photograph is all that you can manage as you leap on and off a tourist bus, or head off to another appointment. It is better to have a quickly taken shot (or series of shots from different angles) than no record at all. You can always delete unsuccessful digital photos later.

However, it is rare for a photograph alone to provide the level of detail and information that may result from a longer observation of a subject, which includes sketching it and adding written notes about form and texture. Sketching involves more time but produces a more developed set of starting points for further work, because the creative side of the observer is engaged and individual responses encouraged, all groundwork to developing your own creative voice.

The tree scar example seen earlier illustrates how a photograph can be used as a starting point. This starting point is developed further in the next chapter, 'Making Marks on Paper.'

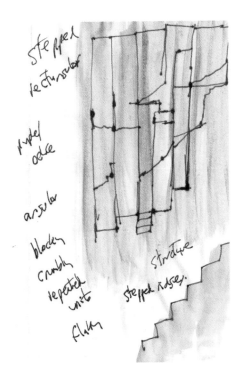

Collecting and storing marks

By developing a collection of marks, your particular interests and recurrent themes will emerge. I collect and file images of a wide variety of marks, because they may be useful to me one day.

Photographs and sketches of marks and the accompanying notes should be stored safely. The ease of taking digital photographs can result in the accumulation of vast numbers of digital images. It is helpful to group these images into folders or files for each of your themes or ideas. My current collection includes images of fixings and fastenings, paths, flowers and plants, and radiating marks. The images are almost entirely of the landscape: I record very few images of people, animals, or urban life, much preferring the seasonality, texture, and richness of the landscape. This preference is part of my personal creative voice.

You may also find it useful to collect photographs from magazines or from the Internet. Images taken from unusual viewpoints, such as from the air, give you a perspective you would not be able to achieve yourself. Newspaper photographs or web images can also record inspiring events that you may never be able to see in real life, such as the Northern Lights in Norway, historic events or places, significant sporting events, or the seasonal migrations of flocks of birds. All this may be useful material for the further development of your stitched textile practice.

Case study: Same mark, different scales

Landscapes sometimes show repeated marks and shapes. This repetition of marks is easy to see in the crystalline structure of rocks, where the crystal's shape is repeated on a larger and larger scale to make the whole object. Exhibits in geological museums show a range of these beautiful crystal structures in fantastic colors.

A similar example of repeated structures in the landscape is the ochre pits in Australia's Northern Territory shown on page 32. A squared rectangular mark is the basic unit of the rock structure and can be observed at large, small, and smaller scales. The rough notes on the accompanying quick sketches shown above left evoke and record key aspects of what I observed.

Above: Initial pen and wash sketches and brief notes on rock structure, colors, and marks, made on site.

Opposite: Rock ridges and layers at the ochre pits, West MacDonnell National Park, Northern Territory, Australia.

4 Making marks on paper

After observing, recording, and collecting marks from different sources, we now turn to developing some of these further as a possible basis for making stitched textiles. Over time, most artists and makers develop and hone their working methods to suit their subject matter, preferred materials, equipment, and working spaces. There are two working methods I have found particularly helpful for developing textile artwork from inspiration, images, and personal sketches. (Information on materials, equipment, and suppliers I have used can be found in the Resources section at the end of the book.)

The first method is to explore thoroughly a chosen set of marks on papers (and sometimes fabrics) using a range of different art media and techniques, before moving on to thinking about stitching. The second method is to move directly to stitching on fabric. The choice between these two methods is often very easy. When I can already visualize the stitch marks I want to use and how they are made, I move directly to working with stitch. More often, I am unsure how to proceed, so I use the first method and start by making paper works related to my source imagery.

Making a range of paper works enables a thorough exploration of your chosen marks, getting to know them in more detail before making stitched samples and then a finished piece of textile work. This type of creative play costs very little in materials and is often great fun. The aim is to create many experiments, knowing that there are no right or wrong outcomes; you are just playing and finding out 'What happens if I do that?' Many of the paperwork techniques covered below can be used effectively on fabrics as well as paper. If fabric seems to suit your purposes better than paper, do try experimenting with it.

Right: Selection of five paper works with resist marks (see page 42).

Initial pen, pencil
and crayon drawings
exploring the marks
on the tree scar
sketchbook pages and
photograph on pages
28 and 29.

Paperwork techniques

Over the time that I have been making textiles, I have developed some specific
techniques for making marks on paper that relate well to stitching and help me
to refine my ideas and thinking. I find that the results translate fairly easily and
reliably into stitched marks. These techniques for drawing and printing are set out
below, with suggestions for further exploration.

For my paper works I use a range of background papers, sometimes in large
(16½ x 23½in or 23½ x 33in) sheets, sometimes working on smaller recycled
pieces of packaging or on previous experiments. Sometimes I use fabrics as well.
Starting work on a pristine piece of paper or fabric can be daunting, but it is good
to experiment with colored or patterned papers or fabrics you have bought, or that
you have colored yourself or recycled from other sources.

Generally, it is easiest to work with a restricted number of colors at this
stage—maybe two or three colors that are related to your source imagery. If you
have a clear sense of the colors you want for a finished textile piece, do use those
colors in your explorations.

The purpose of these explorations is to generate many different sheets of
marks on paper or fabric. It will give you a range of results: some good, some
less so. You can select the best ones later. There may be 'happy accidents' along
the way as you discover that an unexpected combination of paint, paper,
or brushmarks gives just the right effect for your idea.

Preparation

Spread out your sketches, notes, cuttings, and photos in front of you, or pin them
up on a wall in a good light. It is important to be able to refer to them while you
work. The aim is to get to know what works best (and less well) in expressing
your chosen marks to your creative satisfaction. As you copy and repeat the
marks using different techniques, you will notice more about them, and new and
interesting aspects of the marks may become apparent.

Working with pens, pencils, and crayons

Working with pens and pencils is a useful warm-up exercise. We are used to writing by hand using a pen, so this is usually an easy way into developing your ideas. Pens and colored pencils are clean to use, so you can work on your ideas almost anywhere, including while traveling.

Take a good look at your chosen marks and then start by copying, sketching, or tracing them several times. Make sure you notice all the subtleties and fine details of the marks. Then repeat the marks in different sizes and positions on different papers. Try making lines of marks or grids, working on the diagonal or upside down.

Repeat the mark-making processes in different ways and on different papers until you have run out of ideas, or until a really strong idea emerges. The examples shown below and right show an exploration of tree scar marks using different marker pens on cartridge, tracing, and layout papers.

Exploration 7: Alternatives to pencils—calligraphy pens and brushes

Try copying your chosen marks using wide-nibbed calligraphy pens and specialist calligraphy brushes with a range of different inks. These both hold more ink than a conventional pen or brush, and this difference often results in greater subtlety and variability in the marks made.

Exploration 8: Other applicators

There are many other pencil-like applicators worth exploring for mark-making: charcoal, graphite, and water-soluble pastels all offer different effects. Experiment with as wide a range of brushes, sticks, feathers, quills, twigs, and other applicators as possible. Use them with as wide a range of inks, paints, dyes, and pencils as is readily available. Some unexpected combinations can be very effective. The examples shown on page 38 include some lovely subtle and varied marks made by applying sepia calligraphy ink to a rough paper using a dried clematis stem and a twig.

Pen, pencil, and crayon drawings on hand-marbled paper, tracing paper, and layout papers, further exploring the marks of the tree scar photograph on page 29.

Exploration 9: Varying marks

Selection of
paper works from
Explorations 7 and
9 showing marks
made with calligraphy
and larger brushes.
They were made on
large sheets of paper,
working standing up.

Try working with large brushes on bigger sheets of paper or wallpaper placed on the floor (or outside if the weather is suitable), to create larger and bolder marks than is usual for you. Try working standing up, to enable you to vary the pressure you apply to make marks. The examples shown above were made with large brushes and diluted watercolors and inks.

Exploration 10: Varying your working speed

Marks can look very different, depending on how quickly or slowly they were made, so experiment with working at a different pace than is usual for you. For example, John Wolseley, an artist working in Australia, writes of making marks by running with a colleague through the burnt trees left after a forest fire, holding a large piece of paper between them. The resulting paper, with its large-scale, quickly made, complex charcoal marks formed the basis for further work.

Using resists

The use of resists in paper works can create interesting results, which can be translated into stitch. Marks are made with a wax crayon or other water-resistant medium; a diluted water-based medium such as ink or watercolor paint is then washed over the marks. Some examples are shown below and on page 42 and 43.

Exploration 11: Making resist marks

Looking at your chosen marks (pinned or placed where you can easily see them), make marks quickly and firmly with a plain white wax candle on a sheet of white paper. Work standing up if you can, so that you can exert more pressure on the candle as you work and make bolder marks as a result. The white candle and white paper mean that it will be less easy for you to see exactly where you are working and to control the marks you are making. This partial invisibility often results in marks that overlap and create interesting results. For example, the illustration below has overlapping white resist marks made in this way.

When you think you have made enough wax marks to cover the whole sheet of paper, brush a thin coat of well-diluted watercolor or ink over the paper. If the wax was applied firmly enough, the marks will resist the color wash and become clear and distinct against the background (the wash needs to be sufficiently dilute to ensure that the marks resist the color wash and show up clearly).

Exploration 10: An example of a resist made using a white wax candle on white paper.

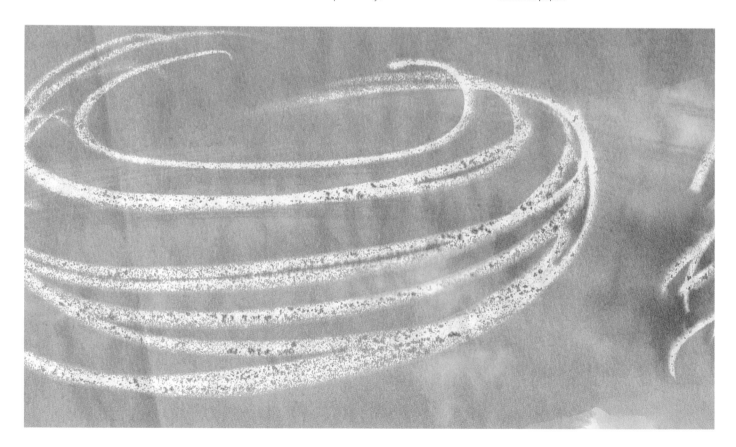

Exploration 12: Using colored resists

Repeat the process on page 41 using colored wax crayons, oil pastels or colored grease pencils to make the resist marks. Then apply a wash made of diluted gouache or acrylic paint over the marks—this usually produces an opaque and more subtle result than ink or watercolor.

Exploration 13: Using other resists

Cut masking tape to length or into small shapes, then apply it to the background paper or fabric using firm finger pressure to form a resist. Brush on a wash of paint or ink and leave the piece to dry. Carefully lift the masking tape pieces away to reveal the background. You can use this method to produce marks with definite edges. This effect can be very useful where a crisp edge to a specific shape is important. At the bottom of the illustration opposite are examples of crisp white shapes on a bright yellow ground and concentric arcs on a green ground.

Right: Resist marks made with various methods. At the top and right is Exploration 12: precise marks made using yellow grease pencil, then washed off with diluted green ink. At the bottom is Exploration 13: two sets of marks made using masking tape as a resist with a colored wash. I used precisely cut shapes of masking tape for the yellow example, and lengths of masking tape for the green one.

Left: Wax resist marks.

Types of printing

Printing is essentially the making of an image by pressing a prepared inked or painted block on to the surface of a selected material. There are many methods of printing on paper and fabric. Prints can be unique, one-off images, known as monoprints, or a sequence of repeated images. We will look at some simple hand-printing techniques for monoprinting and block printing: use them to explore your chosen marks and to provide ideas and insights to develop your personal creative style.

The starting points below will give you some idea of the potential of monoprints for mark-making. The methods can be used on fabrics as well as paper. If you wish to stitch on the fabric later, bear in mind that fabric paints give the most usable results for stitching on. Acrylic paints and water-based oil paints can stiffen fabrics, making them less enjoyable to stitch on.

Monoprinting from finger patterns

Prepare by protecting the worktable with newspaper or a plastic sheet. Place a piece of perspex (or rigid plastic) on the table. Apply an even layer of acrylic paint to the surface of the perspex with a brush. Make marks in the paint using your fingers (wearing gloves if you prefer), working quickly, until you have a set of marks you are ready to print. Place a sheet of paper carefully over the perspex and rub the paper with your fingers, a small hand roller, or a wooden spoon to ensure that the whole print is transferred to the paper. Gently peel away the paper and allow the print to dry. In the illustrations shown left and right, the looping red marks were printed in this way, using water-based oil paints.

Printed marks at various scales. Top: fine, precise yellow marks made using carbon paper (Exploration 14, opposite). Center: two sets of marks from a single monoprint made using a wooden printing block, with additional hand-drawn lines. Bottom and right: Looping marks drawn with fingers into the red printing medium and monoprinted.

Monoprinting from textured surfaces

In the center of the illustration on the opposite page are some fine, greenish marks like wood grain. These marks were produced in the same way as the previous example, except that the base material was wood and not perspex. The wood was covered in paint and the paper inverted on to it. Then parallel lines were drawn on the back of the paper using a wooden spatula. This dual process resulted in two layers of marks: fine marks from the wooden background surface and drawn lines from the spatula marks.

The printing surface can be made from other materials as well as perspex and wood, including textured wallpapers and polystyrene (from food packaging). The printing medium can be acrylic paint (including fabric paints), printing inks, or water-based oil paints. Each combination of printing surface with printing medium creates different challenges in getting a good result, and brings distinct qualities to the final print. Keeping acrylic paint liquid for long enough to make good prints can be tricky, especially if the weather is warm and dry. Water-based oil paints may be more successful, as they are easy to keep workable for longer. However, the prints take longer to dry, which may be a problem if they need to be dried quickly, for example by the end of a workshop. Trial and error will help you decide which printing materials and equipment suit you and your working environment, and produce good results for you.

Exploration 14: Using carbon papers

A further type of monoprint can be made using commercially prepared carbon papers, made for working on paper. Invert the carbon paper over the printing paper and then use a pencil to make marks on the reverse. The result is generally fine, even and precise marks such as those shown in the top of the illustration opposite. Carbon papers are available in a small range of colors—usually blue, red, and gray/black; sometimes yellow.

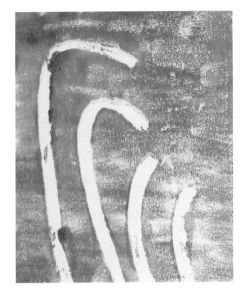  

Above, left to right: First monoprint from the inked styrofoam block, making a well-colored print; styrofoam print block after both prints had been made; Second monoprint taken from the inked styrofoam block, making a much more faintly colored print.

Repeat printing using blocks

Monoprinting can produce great results; however, sometimes a source image or idea calls for the use of a repeated mark or pattern. Block printing techniques can be very useful in this instance. You create a printing surface, known as a block, which can be used more than once. A block is made of durable material and is 'inked' before each print. Readily available materials for blocks include styrofoam and corrugated cardboard, which can be used for small numbers of repeat prints.

Protect the worktable with newspaper or plastic sheet. Place an old towel (or other soft padding), a little bigger than the paper or fabric you wish to print, on the table. Lay the paper or fabric on top, allowing space all around it and ensuring that there are no wrinkles in the padding, paper, or fabric.

Cut a piece of styrofoam to the right size and shape for the block. Looking at your sketches for inspiration, draw marks into the surface of the styrofoam with an old ballpoint pen or a blunt metal tool. It will cut into the styrofoam and create grooves that will hold the printing medium. Styrofoam usually has a grain to it, which makes it difficult to make precise marks in at least one direction, but this adds to the overall effect.

When the marks are made to your satisfaction, brush an even layer of the printing medium on to the surface of the block, avoiding the sides. Invert the block on to the paper or fabric and padding. Smooth the block down with hand pressure or a roller to ensure an even transfer of the printing medium to the paper or fabric. Peel the print away from the block and allow it to dry. At this stage, you can clean the block and reuse it with more medium to make a new print. Alternatively, make further single prints without re-inking—this will produce prints of increasing faintness.

The block can also be inked and applied to the printing paper many times to build up a repeat pattern on all or part of the paper.

A printing block made from recycled styrofoam is shown in the center of the illustration above. The block's design was inspired by the tree scar image seen earlier, and the printing medium is acrylic paint. The left-hand print was the

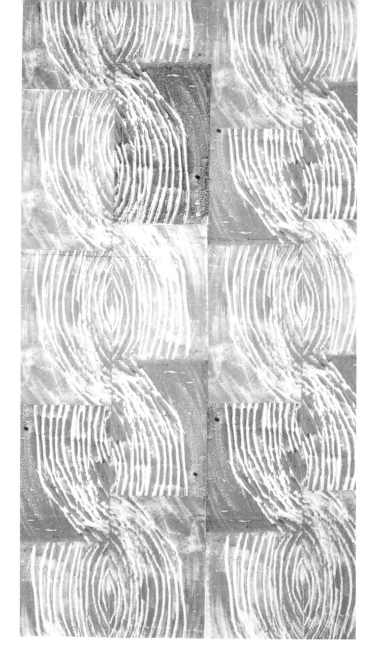

first print taken from the block and it used up most of the printing medium. The right-hand print was the second print taken and it is much fainter because so little printing medium was left. Both prints could be used as a basis for further explorations. Styrofoam blocks can be used to print many times before the grooves degrade, which is useful when working through a range of different color options to develop an idea.

The illustration below right shows a different styrofoam block, inspired by the same tree scar image. I made prints using water-based oil paints in naturally inspired subtle colors. As I was working and repeating this print, it became apparent to me that the pattern of marks that was evolving had further potential. Rather than hand-print more prints and wait for them to dry, I opted for speed. I photocopied one of the prints several times in color. Once I had enough copies, I laid out the prints in different ways to find an arrangement I liked. The resulting layout, shown right, could be adapted further and used for making stitched marks, or as the basis for quilting patterns, or to create block patchwork designs.

Top: Repeat prints from a styrofoam block copied and laid out to develop a repeating pattern. This pattern could be developed further for quilting by hand or machine.

Right: Styrofoam block printing; an example of a simple block is shown at the bottom right, with several prints in subtle colors above and to the left of it.

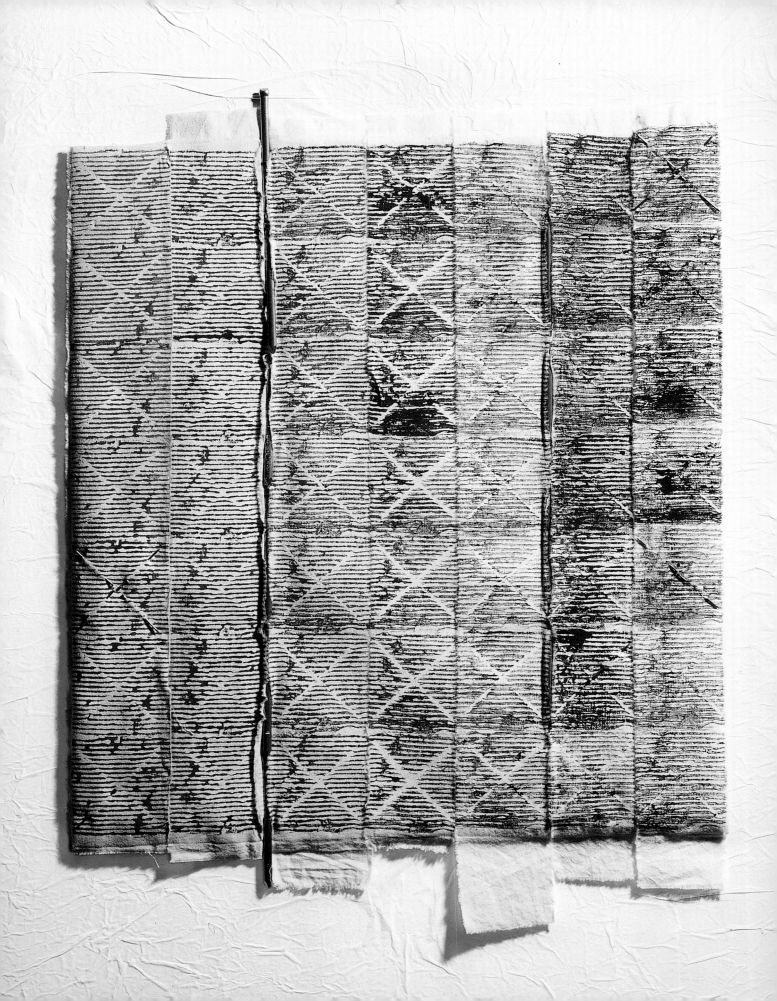

Exploration 15: Cardboard block

Corrugated cardboard provides another interesting surface to use for block printing. As with the wooden surface used earlier, the texture of the cardboard can provide a background texture to a print. With repeated printing, a cardboard block will degrade and poorer-quality images will result. This effect can be employed where a sequence of fainter and more incomplete prints is needed. The illustration opposite shows a textile work constructed from 49 prints of varying densities, created as the cardboard printing block degraded with use. The uneven and varied quality of the prints related well to the absence–presence theme of the piece.

Monoprinting as resist

A further paperwork technique, which has an affinity with stitch, is to use monoprinting and wax crayons and pen marks to create a resist. Begin by covering a sheet of sturdy paper with wax crayon marks, aiming to cover the whole sheet with a thick layer of wax. The crayons can be of many colors, or you may prefer to use a more restricted range of colors, as shown in the illustration below. Here the initial waxed paper sheet was made using only blue, magenta, and turquoise wax crayons.

Then place a sheet of cartridge paper on top of the waxed paper and draw marks on it with a ballpoint pen. The drawn marks need to be made firmly, to ensure that the wax is picked up on the underside of the cartridge paper. When sufficient marks have been made, carefully peel away the cartridge paper from the waxed paper and turn it over to reveal colored wax marks on the underside. When the ballpoint pen marks are drawn with sufficient pressure, they create a raised effect akin to stitch, which can be very useful when designing a stitched textile.

You can further enhance the wax resist marks on the cartridge paper by painting a wash of diluted paint or ink in a toning or contrasting color over them. In the illustration on page 42, the fine curved marks at the top left were made using white paper over the blue, magenta, and turquoise wax crayon sheet seen below. The resist print was washed over with dilute yellow ink, resulting in a series of marks looking very like stitches.

Left: *Absence–Presence,* approx. 84cm x 91cm x 2.5cm (33in x 36in x 1in). Textile/mixed media artwork constructed from 49 individual monoprints on cotton fabric. The prints were made using a corrugated cardboard block with acrylic paint, as set out in Exploration 15.

Right: Waxed paper sheet made using a restricted range of colors.

Exploration 16: Positive and negative prints

Look at both the paper works resulting from this process: a positive print on the reverse of the cartridge paper and a negative print on the waxed sheet. Consider whether one, or both, do justice to your idea. You may want to repeat the technique with different colors of crayon and paint, using colored or more highly textured papers, to get closer to your chosen marks and ideas.

The case study of the development of *Circular Form*, illustrated on pages 110–111, shows this technique in practice. Monoprinted wax resists were used to explore the color, size, and placement of the stitched marks to be used and to consider possible layouts for the finished piece.

Assessing your paper works

Reflection

Once you have a pile of dry paper works developed using the techniques above, gather up any other paper works that seem relevant and pin them all up so that you can see them. You may have the whole of a paper work visible or just the most interesting parts on display. Add your source images for reference if you wish. Ideally, pin up the paper works where you can look at them when you walk past, or where you can sit and look at them for a while.

Stand back and look at the collection and reflect on the marks and your possible choices for further development. Observe which aspects of the paper works attract you and which you dislike. You may find it helpful to consider some or all of the following questions:

- What is visually interesting?
- Are one or two paper works worth more development? If so, which ones? What ideas do you have for their development? Why do those appeal?
- Would changing the size of the marks make a difference?
- Does one paper work link to your original inspiration especially clearly?
- Alternatively, have you found a new angle to explore, which will move you forward from your initial idea? If so, how?
- Look back at your notes to see if your descriptions are best illustrated by one technique and art medium or another. Do you prefer any single technique or particular medium?
- Do you have a clearer sense of the essence of the marks you have chosen now that you have seen different versions? Can you explain this to yourself?
- Can you choose one paper work or part of a paper work to develop further?

Once you have made an initial selection of at least one or two paper works worth further work, store the remainder somewhere safe and out of sight. You may also find it helpful to add to your sketchbook notes at this stage.

For example, while I was exploring the tree scar image on page 29 by making large painted marks, I noticed that the parallel lines of growth around the broken branch were wrapped around the scar itself. The lines bent up at each end in an apparently protective way. My initial sketchbook notes on the photograph had not recorded this wrapping aspect, because I was too excited by the parallel lines to notice anything else. The illustration on the right shows additional written notes on wrapping, reflecting the new insights arising from the paper works stage.

The 'wrapping around' characteristic started a new line of thought for me. I began to consider the idea of wrapping for protection and healing. This idea offered a different and deeper approach to the tree image, moving me on to considering the subject of scars as well the marks and shapes seen. It changed the way I developed the paper works, stitch marks and final textile piece. The illustrations in this section of the book are based on the original photograph of a tree scar.

On reflection, you may find that there is nothing in your paper works that you like, or there may be several different aspects that appeal. If nothing resonates with you at this point, it is worth returning to generating many ideas and marks, perhaps using a different source image or different materials. If you cannot decide which paper work to develop, take a break and return to this aspect of your work later.

Second sets of words:
healing — wrapping — enfolding
damaged — marked — imperfect
linear, parallel lines — strings — cords — stripes
holes — darkness — depth — caves — tunnels

Above: Sketchbook page with tree scar photograph and written notes from a second exploration of the image.

Selection

One of the key skills in making individual textile work is selection. Honing your ability to select only the most worthwhile visual material from your source images and paper works is critical for developing a distinctive approach. From any single visual starting point, individuals are likely to make different artworks. Generally, the more a maker explores and refines her or his ideas, interests and working methods, the more likely the work is to be distinctive and original.

Try to look at your paper works from the same viewpoint as you expect any finished piece to be seen. If you are planning to make a wall-hung textile, pin them up vertically. If you are making a bed quilt, spread them out on a table to get a better idea of how the finished result could appear.

Framing and masking

The images and paper works you are using will have some areas of greater visual interest than others. To explore such areas further, use two L-shaped pieces of black card to create a frame, as shown opposite. Move the frame around, trying out different sizes and shapes. Look at each area you have isolated and see what you think. Does it work? Would a slight move of the frame up or down, or to the left or right, be better? Is a different part of the paper work more interesting? Move it around to select and frame the most visually interesting area or areas.

If you have a specific shape in mind for your finished piece at this stage, it is very useful to use a mask cut to that shape. Do try different shapes: textile artwork does not have to be square or rectangular. Your source idea may be better expressed as a long, thin rectangular landscape, a circle, or some other shape. It can be helpful to use masks made of different-colored cards to make it easier to isolate areas of the paper work. The illustrations opposite show examples of different-shaped masks.

Moving on

Record your experimental framed or masked selections by taking a photograph or making a photocopy of the results. Assemble these selections, stand back, and look again: do you have a way forward yet? If nothing grabs you at this stage, leave the selections pinned up where you can see them as you move around over the next few days. Sometimes the way forward becomes clear when you suddenly notice an aspect of your work in a new light, or from a new angle.

If this process of visual selection seems hard, it may be worth trying to find a word or phrase that describes what you are trying to do and how it feels to you. This can give you a useful insight into your aims in a way that working only with visual materials cannot. Some of the phrases I have used at this stage, for single and multiple pieces of work, are:

- Seeking coherence.
- Telling a visual story.
- Distilling.
- Honing.
- Finding my own view of the world.

- Developing my personal creative voice.
- Making a journey; I have yet to reach my destination, so I need to keep moving on.
- A taming process (like pruning in the garden).
- Growing ideas.

However, sometimes the paper works do not work out as you have envisioned, despite your best efforts. If that happens, try making another set of paper works, using a different technique and art medium. Alternatively, take a break and come back to your work another time. It can be tempting to force yourself to make a decision, but making art textiles can be much more satisfying if the various stages and processes are reflective and enjoyable rather than rushed.

Above and right: Examples of different-shaped masks including L-shaped frames, overlaid onto a paperwork of colored marks to enable areas of visual interest to be isolated for further work.

5 Making stitch marks

You may approach this part of the book having worked through the previous chapter and selected one or part of one of your paper works that you feel has potential to be developed further. Alternatively, you may have chosen to work directly with making stitch marks.

Working on paper or fabric with art media can clarify much of the thinking needed to make a textile piece. However, there are aspects of working in textiles that can only be understood, felt, and developed by experimenting and working directly with fabrics and threads. It is important to include the development of stitch marks within the design process to take account of the special qualities of textiles, rather than working entirely on paper to develop your ideas. For many makers, including myself, stitching is often the most exciting stage.

When working with stitch, and with quilting in particular, there is a synergy that comes when layers of fabrics are stitched through and come together into a new form. As the chosen hand-stitched or machine-stitched marks cover the fabric, they create a new textile, which is more than the sum of its individual parts. This new textile can only be achieved by stitching, often quite densely or in a very specific way. It is this almost magical transformation that makes working in stitched and quilted textiles so enjoyable.

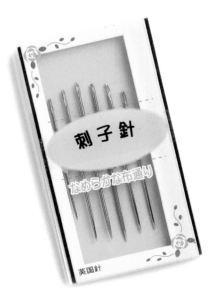

Left: Japanese sashiko needles.

Right: Detail of spiral quilting hand-stitched on silk fabrics with silk batting. The piece was stitched first, then dyed using pink and grey fiber-reactive dyes.

Hand- and machine-stitched marks and lines

To me, one of the key differences in textiles is between hand-stitched marks and lines and machine-stitched marks and lines. This difference is shown above and opposite, in a sample based on a design in a children's coloring book. The hand-stitched marks are a broken dashed line, whereas the machined marks make a solid line. This difference means that a machined line is generally visually harder and stronger than a hand-sewn one. The illustration above shows a painted symbol softly outlined with hand stitches and then echoed by widening lines of machine stitch, which appear quite hard and distinct. Of course, it is possible to vary both hand- and machine-stitched marks to show other qualities. For example, a line of backstitch quilting in a dark, thick thread can make a strong visual line, and machine stitches can be made that are both delicate and separate.

The choice of stitching method, together with the fabrics used, also affects the feel of a finished textile. Usually, working with machined marks produces a stiffer overall result than working with hand-stitched marks, especially when the stitches are massed. Fabric choice also has an important influence on the results. For example, massed machine stitch on layers of butter muslin can create a soft and draped texture, which can then be stiffened if paint or other media are applied. However, it is often easiest and most enjoyable to work with the inherent qualities of the fabrics and stitch techniques rather than against them.

There are many ways to translate marks and ideas into stitched textiles. In this section of the book, we look at some of the possibilities, starting with running stitch and some variations, including spirals and loops, and then various stitches derived from knots, some of which are inspired by embroidery stitches, including French knots. Many of the samples shown are influenced by English North Country quilting.

Above: Hand-painted abstract symbol outlined in hand stitch, then echo-quilted by machine in lines that are increasingly widely spaced.

Opposite: Design based on a children's coloring book and stitched partly by hand and partly by machine.

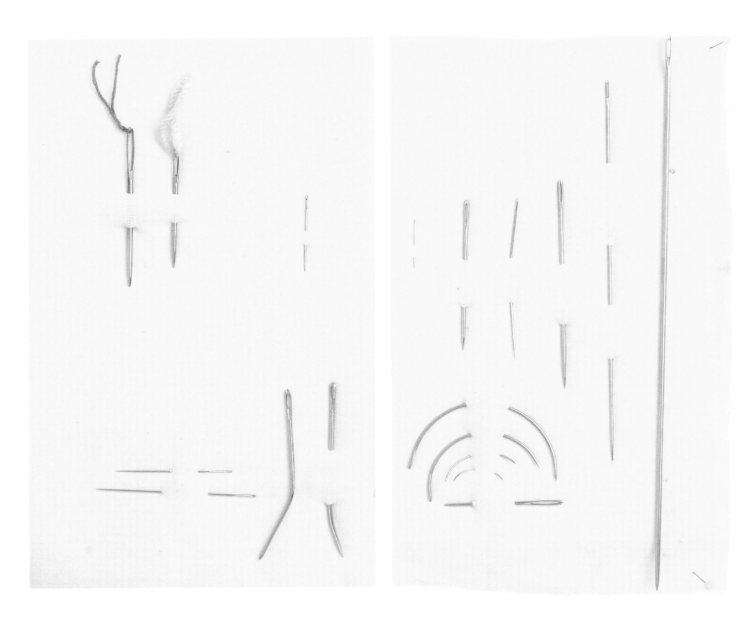

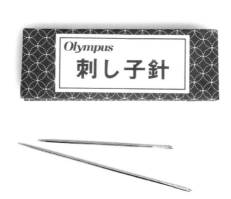

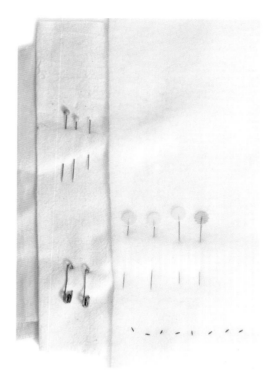

Left: Selection of ways to secure layers of fabrics before stitching (top to bottom, left to right): different-sized glass-headed pins, safety pins, yellow flower pins, and at bottom right a line of black tacks from a quilters' tacking gun.

Choosing needles and threads

Above left: A selection of hand sewing needles on a yellow cloth background. Top row: Tapestry needles in two sizes, 'between' needles for fine quilting stitches, long darners, and a mattress needle. Bottom row: a beading needle, bent needles, and curved surgical and upholstery needles.

Left: a vintage packet of needles, Japanese sashiko needles, and a set of tapestry needles.

When making stitch marks, working by either hand or machine, the first decision to make is about needle and thread. A careful consideration of which needle and thread combination best suits the idea, purpose, and the maker is important, as it helps to ensure that the textile will be an enjoyable piece of work to make and satisfying when completed. Much of the work in this book was made using a long, strong needle known as a long darner, because that suited the kind of stitch mark I wanted to make and it was easy and physically comfortable to use for long periods of time.

Traditional hand-quilted work was often made using a strong thread and a small needle, for the characteristic fine and even stitch marks. Contemporary textile work is usually made using a wider range of combinations of fabrics, threads and needles to achieve particular effects. Many textile artists make very distinctive stitch marks in their work as a result.

As you experiment, you will find that some combinations of needles, threads, and fabrics suit you and your ideas better than others. The key is to explore as many options as you can. The illustration on page 61 shows a range of hand-sewing needles and a line of running stitch made with each, using a thread of suitable thickness for the eye. The variety of stitch marks that can be made from this simple starting point is extensive.

Exploration 17: Sampling needles and threads

Gather a selection of hand-sewing needles and threads. Select a suitably sized plain cotton fabric and place it on top of a layer of thin batting cut to the same size as the fabric. Add a backing layer of the same cotton fabric, or a lightweight fabric such as muslin. Pin the layers to secure them, using long, glass-headed pins or curved safety pins. Tack the layers together if you prefer.

To begin with, work in hand stitch, using a medium needle, with an eye large enough to make threading the needle straightforward (and not so large that the thread falls out during stitching). Start by stitching lines of regular stitches across the sample, making them all small or all large stitches, for example.

Then try different combinations of needles, threads and stitch sizes. As you experiment, see which personal preferences emerge. Do you find using a small needle and making small, regular stitches with an even tension easy to do, or is using a larger needle and making a bolder mark more your style? Experiment further: for example, if making bold stitch marks suited you, try working with even larger needles and thicker threads. As you cover the fabrics with stitches, notice how the layers become more integrated.

A wide range of needles can be found at specialist suppliers (see page 122), and it can be fun to explore working with them. Each will produce different stitch marks and some needles are much easier to use than others.

Below: More examples of specialist needles: bookbinders' needles, sailmakers' needles, and a pack of tiny betweens needles.

Right: Range of hand sewing needles and a line of running stitch made with each needle using black thread of suitable thickness for the eye. The needles shown are (from left to right): three different long darners, a beading needle, three domestic sewing sharps, a leather needle (which has a triangular point), and three traditional quilting needles.

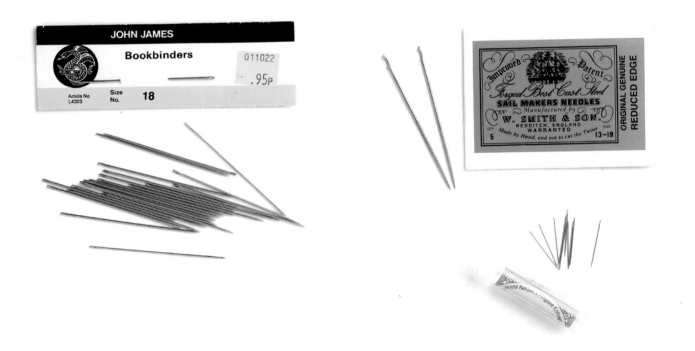

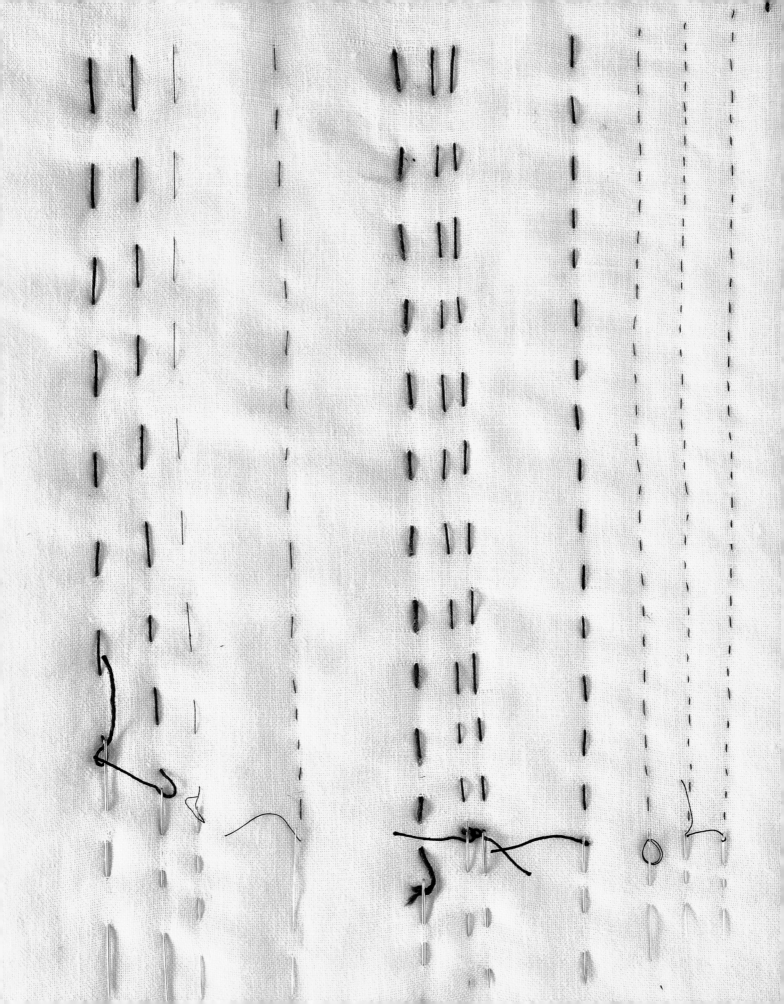

Hand-stitched marks

This section of the book discusses some of many possible techniques you can use to create hand-stitched marks: running stitch, radiant stitch, spiral stitch, loop stitch, reef knots and ties, and French knots.

Running stitch

Running stitch is a basic hand stitch, offering many variations and applications. The examples shown on page 64 give an idea of the variations possible when individuals of various ages are given a wide variety of needles and threads to make their own exploration of running stitch. The use of color and overstitching adds further visual complexity to the basic process of stitching.

How to do running stitch

1. Secure the thread on the back of the fabric(s) by making a couple of small anchoring stitches, or by using a knot.
2. Bring needle and thread up at A (see below).
3. Insert needle and thread at B and pull through to the back, leaving a smooth stitch.
4. Bringing the needle and thread up at C and then down again at D, to make the next stitch. Repeat the stitch bringing the needle and thread up at E and down at F.
5. Continue making stitches, working from left to right, and keeping the tension smooth and even.
6. Experiment with making further lines of running stitch, varying the lengths of the stitches to obtain different effects.
7. Experiment with making further lines of running stitch, this time varying the spacings between the lines and exploring making the knots at the start of the thread visible.

Opposite: Successive layers of colored running stitch lines, stitched by hand using different needles and thread types and thicknesses. On the left-hand side of the sample additional running stitch lines of small, regular purple stitches give a flatter and more integrated appearance.

A B C D E F

Direction of stitch →

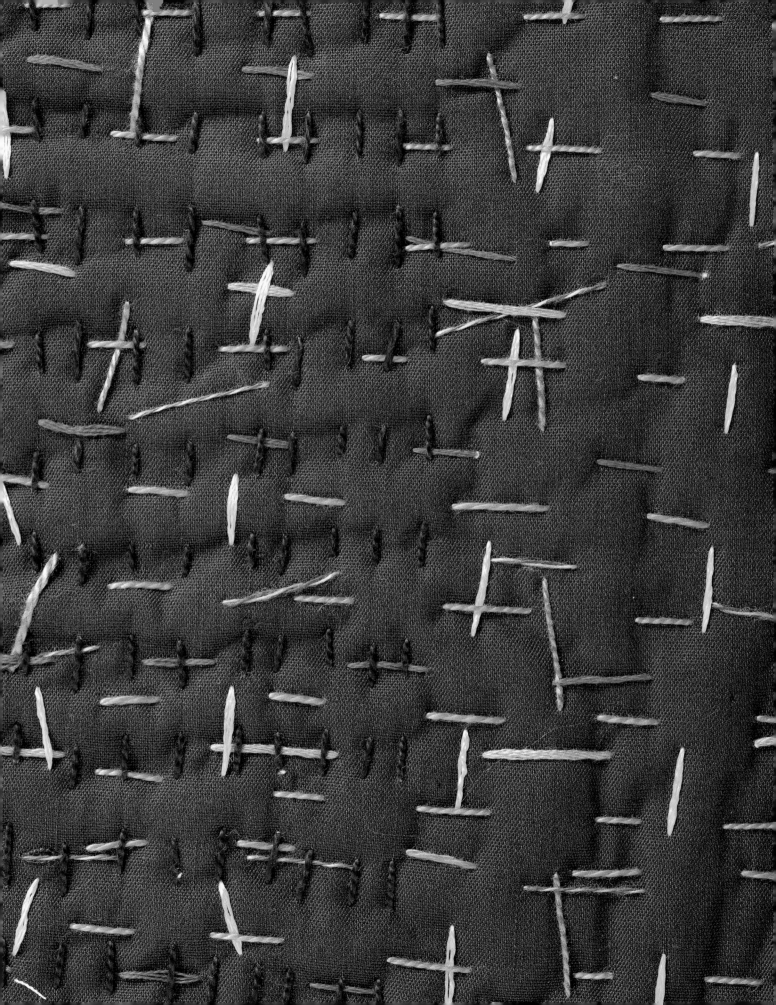

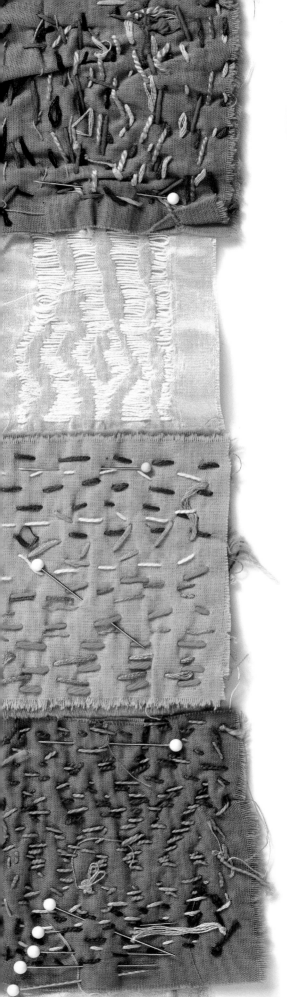

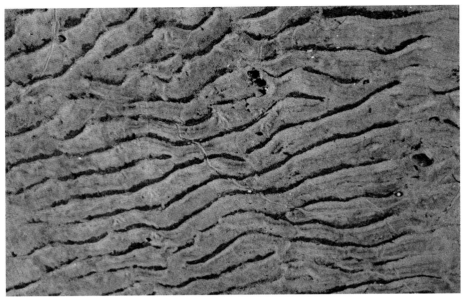

Case study: Working from sources to make stitch marks

Over the years I had collected a wide range of photographs of beaches, such as the one shown above. Some of them had been developed into paper works, although the way forward to making completed textile artworks continued to elude and daunt me. The processes of making the paper works had ensured that I had become very familiar with my subject matter, and I knew that I wanted to work with the idea of sand ripples to make large-scale textile artworks. The breakthrough came when I was exploring working with fabric layers and hand stitch one day. It occurred to me that basic running stitch might be effective if it was worked in parallel lines over the whole fabric's surface. I discovered that as the fabric layers were covered by parallel lines of stitch, the fabric started to ripple. The small sample shown opposite was stitched on layers of random-dyed cotton fabric, with ordinary sewing thread and a medium needle. This initial sample was enough to enable me to see the potential of making larger, more controlled stitch marks. When individual stitches are made more systematically, the rippling effect can be controlled and shaped ridges made selectively. This led to a long series of textile works, for example *Shifting Sands VII* on page 13.

Left: Some examples of running stitch marks sewn by people of different ages and skill levels, showing some of the many variations that can be made on the basic hand-stitched mark.

Above: Beach sand ripples, Isle of Arran, Scotland.

Right: *Ripples*—first experimental sample, hand-stitched on dyed cotton fabrics using machine sewing thread.

Radiant stitch

A simple running stitch line can be applied in many ways. In traditional North Country hand quilting, stitching is begun in the center of a piece and then worked outwards. This helps to ensure that the final textile is as smooth and wrinkle-free as possible, and has an even tension. My research into this way of working led me to make a piece of textile artwork influenced by this method.

In your files you may have images or sketches where the marks or shapes radiate outwards in some way. Examples from my collection are shown opposite.

Using your chosen fabric, thread, and needle, build up a series of lines, each starting in the center and working outwards in the radial pattern set out below. The illustration on page 68 shows some further stitched samples inspired by spiral growth patterns, composite flower heads, and Ordnance Survey map symbols, which could be used to develop a finished piece of textile work.

How to do radiant stitch

Clockwise from top left: Harbor post, Whitby; sawn tree trunk; goat's beard flower, Baslow, Derbyshire; star pavement mark, Bents Green, Sheffield; drain cover, St Ives, Cornwall (center); plant with star-shaped flowers, Padley Chapel, Derbyshire.

1. Starting from the center and working outwards, stitch the lines in numerical order, starting at 1, using running stitch. Then stitch the quarter division lines (lines 2, 3, and 4 on the diagram).
2. Add further rows of stitch, always bisecting the space left between two rows to keep an even tension.
3. Continue to add more lines of stitch, bisecting the remaining spaces, until the work is sufficiently stitched.

Note: The placement of the lines of stitches was judged by eye. The lines could be marked out before stitching if that is helpful.

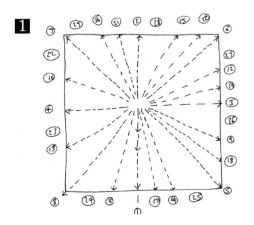

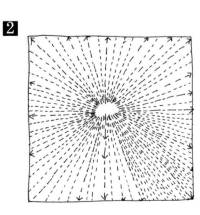

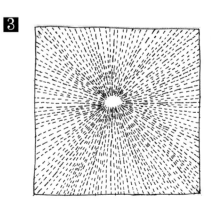

Samples of radiant stitch. Top left: Red spiral sample used to develop the finished piece Red Radiant. Top right: Radiant stitch 'flowers'. Bottom: Radiant stitch marks inspired by the symbols used on Ordnance Survey maps.

Spiral stitch

A further application of running stitch is to stitch lines in spirals, each worked outwards from a different central point, as shown in the diagrams on page 70. These spiral marks work best when stitched on layers of fabric, or fabric with batting, to provide the necessary stability. They can be used to provide a subtle background texture in a quilt, for example by using a thread close in color to that of the fabric. Or you can use a vibrantly colored plain or variegated thread to make the spiral mark itself visible as well as creating a texture.

The extent of the stitched spirals and the size and tension of each stitch will all contribute to the depth of the spirals. Keeping a tight tension on the thread and using small stitches to sew small spirals can produce a strongly textured result. Conversely, a large spiral mark, made with larger stitches worked at normal tension, can produce a flat spiral with minimal texture. The samples on page 55 and below were worked on different silk fabrics and dyed after the stitching was completed.

Spiral quilting in different-sized spirals worked with a light, even tension, leaving some areas unstitched.

How to do spiral stitch

1. Working on two or three layers of fabric, secure the thread on the back by making a couple of small anchoring stitches, or by using a knot.
2. Bring the needle and thread up through the fabrics at the center of the first spiral stitch, at A.
3. Make a couple of small running stitches to begin the spiral. Turn the fabric clockwise as you stitch, to ensure a smoothly curved spiral. At the start of a stitching it is easiest to turn the fabrics after each stitch.
4. Carry on stitching clockwise around the spiral, pulling the thread through carefully each time to leave a smooth stitch.
5. Carry on stitching around the spiral until you reach the desired size.
6. Take needle and thread through to the back of the fabric and make a couple of small anchoring stitches.
7. Bring the needle and thread up at the center of the next spiral. Moving to the center of the next spiral can be done neatly by taking the thread between the fabric layers, rather than leaving the thread visible on the back.
8. Continue making spiral stitches across all, or selected parts of, the fabric surfaces, keeping the tension light for a flat effect. For a more textured effect, work with a tighter tension to raise the spirals as you work.
9. Explore the potential of making spiral stitches by using different thicknesses of thread, making different sizes of spiral and exploring where they are best placed on the work.

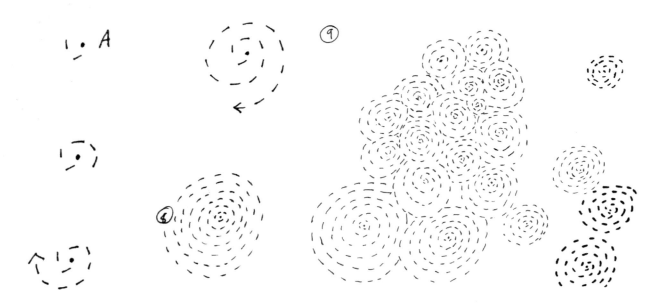

Loop stitch

Running stitch can be adapted to create loops from individual stitches as they are made. As each stitch is taken, the thread is not pulled completely through; some thread is retained each time to make a loop. The retention of more thread creates a larger loop. Each loop needs to be anchored at the back with small stitches to ensure that it remains the chosen size and does not pull out.

A careful choice of thread and fabric can result in interesting and varied looped marks that are raised away from the surface of the textile. This loop stitch works best with strong, thick threads, which have sufficient strength to stand away from the fabric and remain standing when made into loops. Linen bookbinding thread or similar seems to work particularly well. Not all threads suit this type of mark-making stitch, and experimentation is essential to achieve good results. Some examples of loop-stitch marks using alternative combinations of fabric and thread are shown on the right. *Surface Interventions* (page 77) shows loop stitch marks used to make a large-scale piece.

How to do loop stitch

1. Secure the thread on the back of the fabric(s) by making a couple of small anchoring stitches, or by using a knot.
2. Bring the needle and thread up at A. Insert the needle and thread at B and pull through to the back, leaving a loop of thread of the chosen size on the front, thus making the loop stitch.
3. Secure the loop stitch on the back with a couple of small anchoring stitches to prevent it being pulled out of size and shape.
4. Bring the needle and thread up at C, make another loop and then take the needle down at D. Secure the loop stitch on the back with anchoring stitches. Repeat by bringing the needle and thread up at E, making a loop and taking the needle and thread down at F. Make small stitches to secure each loop.
5. Continue making loop stitches, working from left to right, and keeping the loops the same size.
6. Experiment by making further lines of stitch with varied sizes of loop and spacings of stitch.

A B C D E F

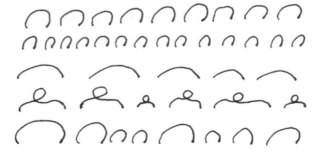

Right: Samples of loop stitch worked in a range of threads on different fabrics. From top: linen thread and metallic thread, random-dyed blue/white cotton thread, scarlet fibre reactive-dyed thread, black shirring elastic, linen threads.

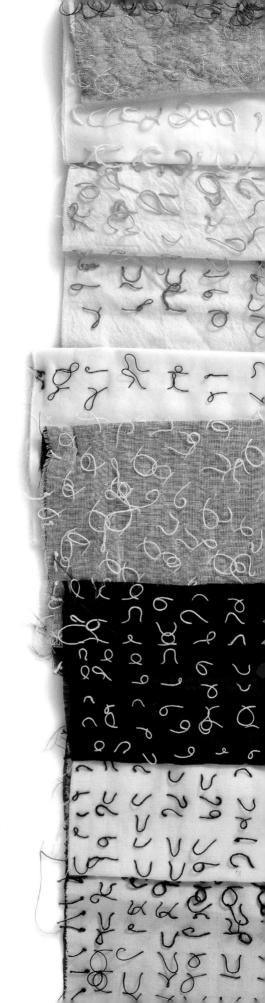

Knots

Left: Selection of layouts for *Field Path (Buttercups)*. The completed piece is shown on the right.

Knots offer a visually intriguing stitch mark with interesting symbolic value. For example, it was traditional to tie a knot in the corner of a handkerchief to remember something, or we may speak of a 'knotty problem,' meaning something difficult to resolve. Knots are also found in designs, for example English knot gardens, and in historical sources such as Celtic manuscripts. Of course knots also have a practical purpose, and some working examples from a harbor are shown below. In textile work, knots can hold layers of fabric together temporarily, or form a permanent part of a completed piece of work.

Many types of knot can be adapted for use in textile work. We will look only at reef knots and French knots here, but a book on knots will help you to explore the subject further. A good reference book should provide details of such delights as slipknots, marine knots, the bowline, the executioner's knot and the intricate Chinese knots used in festival and special-occasion decorations, among others.

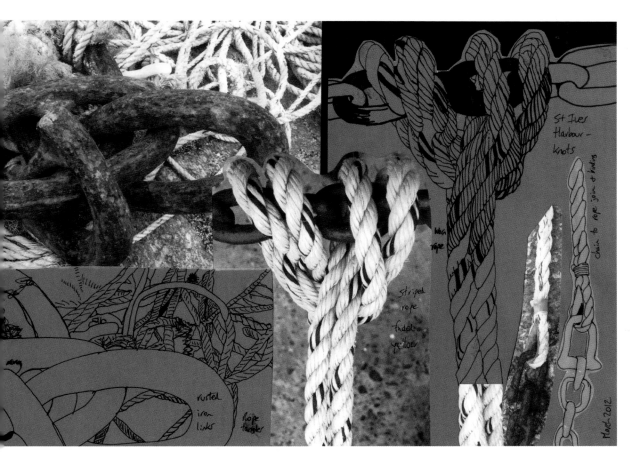

Above: Paper work developed from photographs of knots taken at St Ives fishing harbor, Cornwall.

Right: *Field Path (Buttercups),* 13cm x 89cm x 4 cm (5in x 35in x 1½ in).

Sunshine and Shadow, 122cm x 122cm
(48in x 48in). Calico and linen thread.

Simple knots often occur in hand sewing, as we may make a knot at the end of a thread to secure it before beginning to stitch. When knots are visible on the surface of a piece of textile artwork, rather than hidden on the reverse as is usual, they can be very versatile marks in their own right. *Room to Roam* (see page 25) combines parallel lines of hand-made running stitch with lines of simple knots to bold effect.

Reef knots and ties

Reef knots can be used to tie fabric layers together. Knots can be made more quickly and easily than sewing the layers together and are probably more likely to appear on functional items made for day-to-day use, such as quilts, than on decorative pieces of work. A utilitarian knot can become visible and even decorative on occasion.

Reef knots are best made with strong threads, using a sturdy needle to stitch through all the layers of fabric (or fabric and batting). Once the stitch has been made where it is needed, pull the thread through and cut it, leaving sufficient thread on both sides of the stitch to enable you to tie the knot securely and easily. To make a secure knot it is important to have sufficient thread to work with. Cut the ends of the thread to a length that suits the piece of work. It is sometimes helpful to make two reef knots, one on top of the other, for a bolder mark.

Knots can be made at differing densities across the fabric, like a pencil drawing that is shaded more heavily in some areas. The illustration below shows areas with a light and heavier density of stitch marks, from a corner of the textile piece *Sunshine and Shadow,* shown opposite.

Below: Corner detail of *Sunshine and Shadow* (left) showing the increasing density of the knotted marks.

As with any stitch, knots can be varied by changing the fiber of the thread, altering the thickness and colors of the threads and the length of the thread tails. The illustration on page 4 shows how different thicknesses of thread were used to change the look of stitch marks. The black linen thread makes a far more visible mark than the wispy and subtle black domestic sewing thread. The red crochet thread is of an intermediate thickness and makes a highly visible mark because of its color.

How to do a reef knot

1. Insert needle and thread down through all the fabric layers and bring back to front of fabrics, making a stitch.
2. Cut threads to length, ensuring enough thread to make a secure knot easily.
3. Place left thread over right thread and tuck under.
4. Now place the thread on the right side over the thread on the left and tuck under.
5. Pull the thread ends to make the knot neat and even.
6. Cut the thread ends to the correct size for the piece of textile work.

Surface Interventions,
6½ft x 6½ft (2m x 2m).
Hand-stitched in loop
stitch with black linen
thread on layers of calico.

French knot samples. Left: French knots used to
secure small green cotton sateen squares to a muslin
and batting background. Right: sample made as
development for *Field Path (Buttercups)* (finished piece
shown on page 73). Also shown is a hand-colored
cotton thread bundle.

French knots

A French knot is used in embroidery to provide a dot. It is a decorative, textural stitch mark, generally not suited to functional textile pieces. The knot is created by wrapping thread around the needle once and then inserting the needle close by and pulling it carefully through to the reverse side of the fabric. It may take a little practice to achieve this mark consistently, with some interesting variations along the way. A bolder knot mark can be created by wrapping the thread around the needle three or four times before pulling the needle even more carefully through to the reverse of the piece.

As with previous techniques, varying the threads and fabrics used can create a range of bold and subtle marks to suit your purposes. Some examples are shown on the right. Possible sources of inspiration for working with French knots can be seen on page 81.

How to do French knots

1

2

3

1. Bring the needle and thread up at point A. Wrap the thread once around the needle.

2. Take down at point A, or close to it.

3. Gently pull the thread through to make a neat knot.

Examples of French knots worked with different threads on linen and paper.

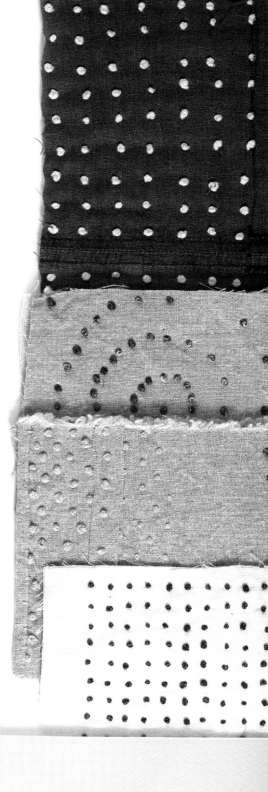

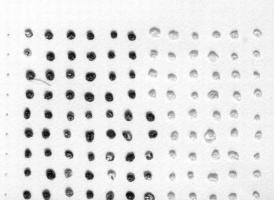

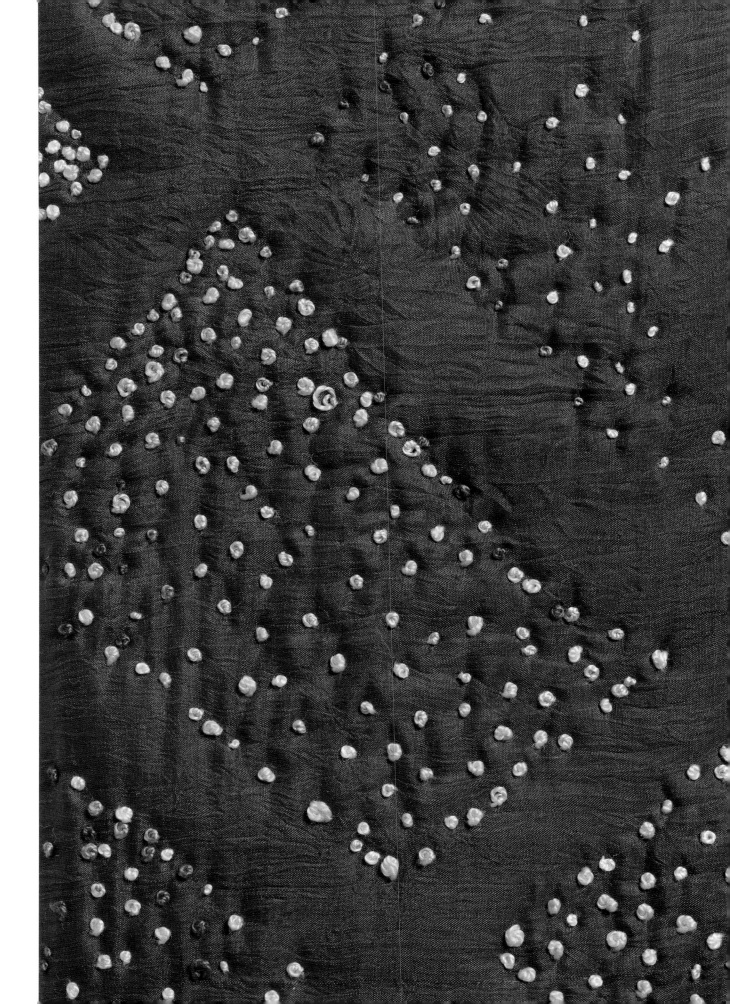

Case study: Using French knots

The little pen sketches shown on the right were drawn quickly from memory after walking in local fields. The fields are criss-crossed by much-walked paths originally related to mining and the lead trade. The sense of the antiquity and continuity of people walking in this landscape interested me. In addition, the field itself and the paths across it vary visually with the seasons. In March, the field is mostly a grassy green with green paths, then many buttercups grow on the untrodden areas and flower in vibrant yellows; a few months later the buttercups die back and the grass turns a late summer green, then turns to the darker bronze-green of autumn, broken by brown, muddy paths. Sometimes, in winter, everywhere is covered by brilliant white snow, with the paths only showing as subtle changes in the level of the ground. I see this field often and I wanted to use repeated knotted stitch marks to evoke my memories of walking on the paths and seeing the buttercups in flower.

Working from my original sketchbook drawings with my computer and printer, I laid out and printed multiple copies and multiple selections. Some of the layouts are shown on page 72. The layouts with more cross marks seemed to offer the most potential for development. The final layout was chosen to suit the long, thin format of the wooden stretcher. The completed piece is shown on page 73 and a detail shown opposite.

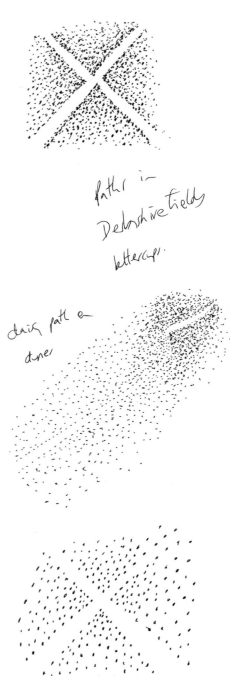

Left: Detail of *Field Path (Buttercups)* showing different-sized French knots.

Above: Inspiration for using French knots: early spring leaf buds on branches and some related sketches.

Quick sketches from memories of walks. Top: Paths in a buttercup field. Lower: Path through daisies on a grassy sand dune.

Machine-stitched marks

Many of the hand-stitched marks explored earlier can be copied or adapted for machining. More interestingly, machine-stitched marks have unique qualities that can be used to create distinctive results. These include the ease of making continuous lines of marks, covering textile surfaces densely with one or more layers of marks, and the ability to work on a larger scale. Machine-stitched marks can look almost like a drawing and may be suited to realizing a hand-drawn quality in your textile work. More practically, using a sewing machine is often quicker than working by hand. Machine stitching and quilting can be used to produce durable, washable textiles that are suited to regular use. The earlier comments about the importance of choosing an appropriate size of needle and thickness of thread apply here too. A machine needle should also be the correct type for the fabric being used.

Machine embroidery is a wide field and there are many books that will teach you more about it. A good starting point is *Machine Embroidery Stitch Techniques* by Val Campbell-Harding and Pamela Watts.

Free-machined marks

With a modern sewing machine, you can make machine-stitched marks with the feed dogs either up or down. Working with the feed dogs up, as in conventional machine sewing, can be useful when a consistent tension, regularity, or quality of line is needed, for example when durability is important. Free machining means stitching with the feed dogs down and a zero setting for stitch length. This arrangement puts the user entirely in charge of the marks being stitched. Free machining has been used on the machine-stitched samples throughout the book. The instruction booklet for your sewing machine may answer any questions you have about free-machining technique and maintenance of the machine. For further ideas and inspiration for machine stitch and embroidery, see the Bibliography on page 127.

We are going to look at the some of the many variations on basic free-machine stitching technique: single marks, massed marks, all-over stitch marks, continuous marks, layered marks, and dots, webs, and tufts. All these free-machine stitch marks can be explored and developed by changing the threads and fabrics, by layering them, changing their placement, or combining them. The examples shown right and on pages 84 and 85 are starting points.

Right: Sample of free-machine stitching on hand-dyed fabric, based on a pebble beach.

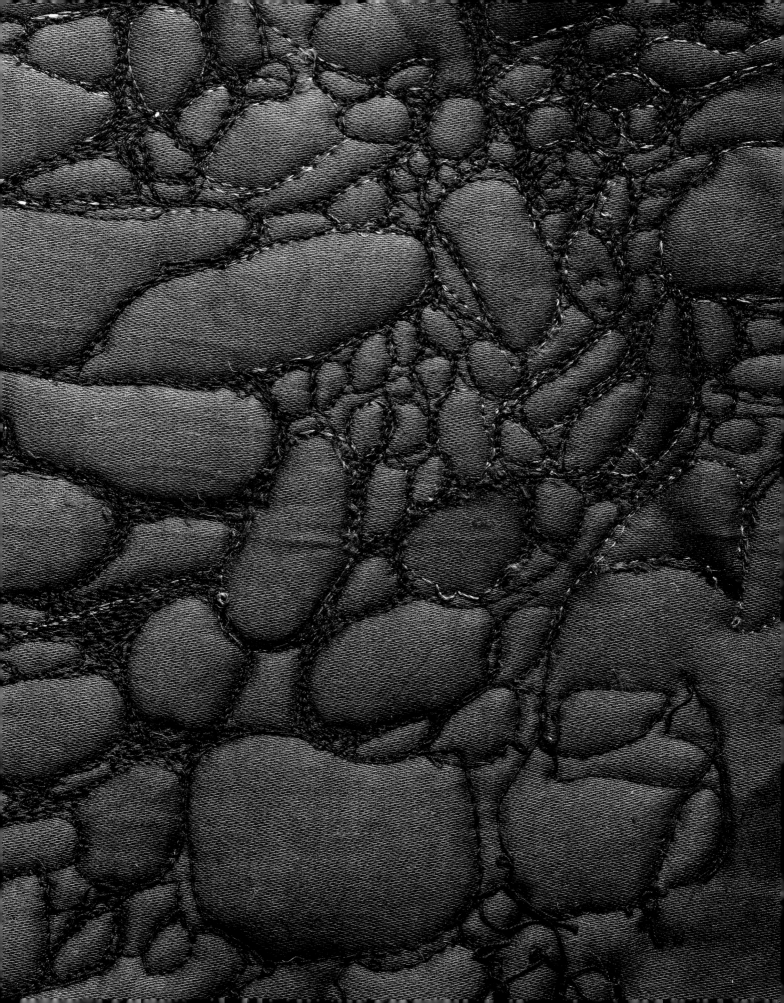

Single marks

Single marks can be repeated at varying sizes and spacings to give a wide variety of results. In the example below, the stitching was worked from the center of each spiral outwards. Each spiral was started with a few small stitches made on top of each other to anchor the thread. Then the stitching was worked outwards, turning the fabric as needed to obtain a good spiral shape. When the correct size of spiral mark was achieved, the needle was lifted and the fabric moved to enable the needle to be brought down in the center of the next spiral to be stitched. (When experimenting with this stitch mark, you may find it easier to mark the center points of all the spirals with chalk or washable marker pen before starting to stitch.) When the stitching of all the spirals was complete, the connecting threads were mostly cut away. Because this was a sample, a few connecting threads were left in place to show how the stitch mark differs with these extra lines present.

Simple marks can be layered and their sizes varied to suit the textile artwork. The illustration on the left shows simple star marks in several sizes. They have been stitched in variegated thread, with the long connecting threads left in some areas. This sample was worked quickly, like doodles or sketches. The aim was to record the idea quickly, maybe for use later. Further exploration of the colors of both fabric and threads, and more thought and planning in the placement of the stitch marks, could produce some worthwhile results from the initial simple mark.

Machine-stitched marks can also be used to 'draw' on fabric (as shown on page 83). This sample was inspired by a magazine photograph of a wet shingle beach at low tide. It was made on hand-dyed cotton sateen, with the stitches outlining the shapes of the pebbles.

Right: Machine-stitched star marks with and without connecting threads in place.

Below: Machine-stitched spiral marks.

Massed stitch marks

As noted earlier, machine-stitched marks can be built up to cover a surface very densely, possibly leaving very little or none of the background fabric visible. Such massed stitch marks can also be used to raise or flatten specific areas of a textile work. The examples below and on pages 86, 87, and 88 show three of many possible effects that can be achieved.

Right: This fabric was block-printed by hand with fabric paint using the corrugated cardboard block seen in the artwork on page 48, then machine-stitched selectively with white lines to flatten areas and push the cross shapes upwards.

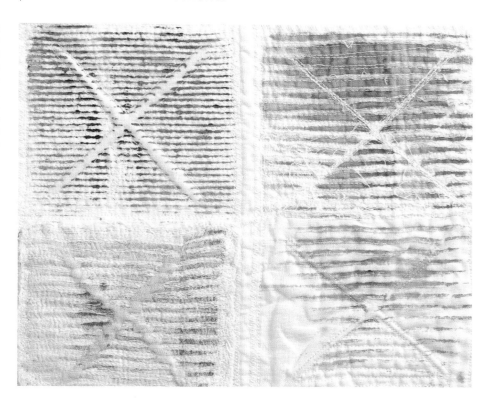

Right: Massed stitch lines worked diagonally onto fabric (with batting underneath) to flatten small square areas and to raise the fabric into a grid.

Massed machine-stitched marks work well on layered fabric pieces, such as quilts, to create areas of texture and definition. The *Cup and Ring 1* wall hanging (see page 2) is heavily machine-stitched in lines across much of the surface to flatten and quilt large areas, and to raise and define smaller rounded areas as part of the overall design. The hanging is quite heavy and stiff as a result of the massed machine stitching and the use of a woollen blanket as batting.

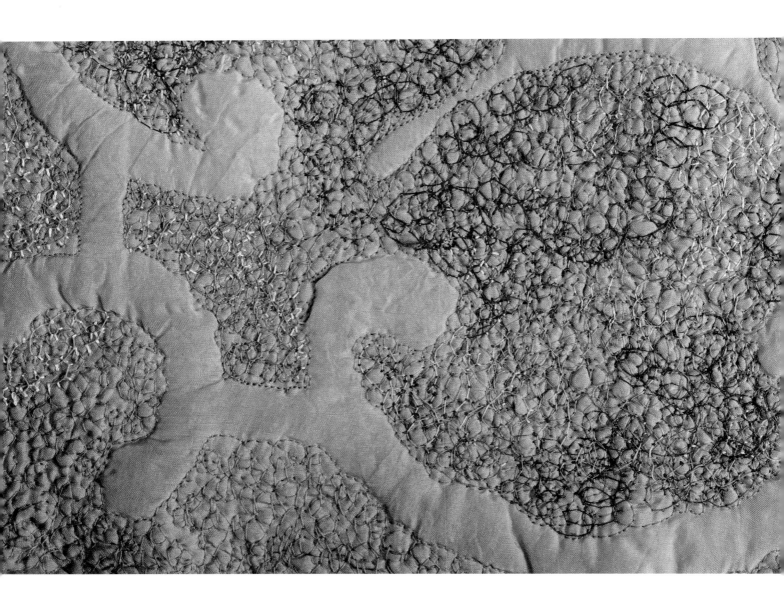

A formal knot garden design stitched in massed curves of machine stitch. The tension of the stitching was altered to pull the colored bobbin thread through to the front of the piece providing additional surface color. In machine embroidery this technique is also known as whip stitch. Detail shown opposite.

All-over stitch marks

Machine-stitched marks can also be worked evenly over the surface of a textile piece to bond the fabric layers and create a durable finish. The illustration below shows the use of an all-over curved stitch mark in red thread on a cream calico ground. The calico was then brushed with varying densities of red acrylic textile paint. In some places, the paint and thread together have created a red surface; in other places, the paint touched only the raised areas between the stitches, leaving a mottled finish. Again, further planning and exploration, including more controlled application of paint on the stitched areas, could provide some interesting results.

All-over stitch marks, worked densely, can be used to finish the edges of textile pieces, potentially providing a durable and visually integrated edge with a contemporary feel. Much contemporary stitched textile work does not have borders at the edges, like the ones found on many traditionally made pieced quilts. The illustration on page 108 shows an example of such a contemporary edge.

Right: All-over curved stitch marks in red thread on a cream calico ground (with batting underneath). The calico surface was then brushed with varying densities of red acrylic textile paint. In some places the paint and thread together have merged and created a red surface. In other places the paint touched only the raised areas between the stitches, leaving a mottled cream and red finish.

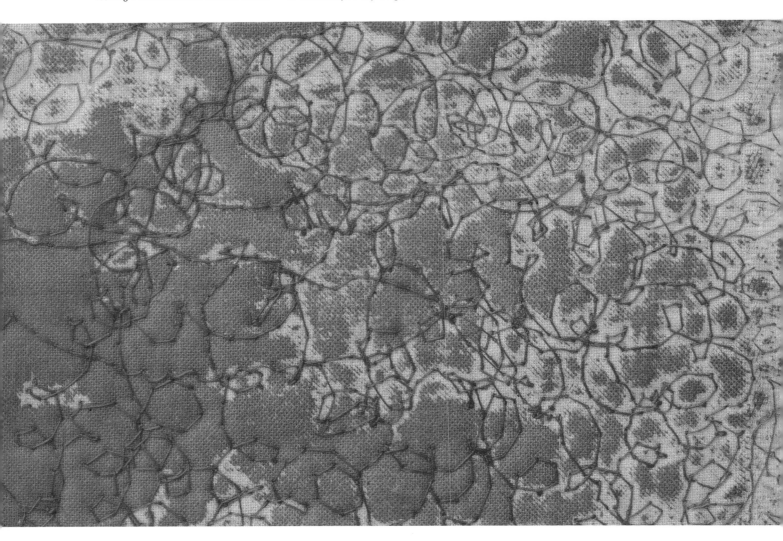

Continuous lines

One of the most exciting and distinctive aspects of machine stitching is the ease with which you can make continuously stitched marks. These can be simple straight or curved lines, or made of single motifs joined into lines. The example below provides some starting points. The initial doodles on yellow paper show some ideas for lines of stitch marks. These ideas have been translated directly into machine-stitched marks, using a dark green thread on a background of pale green cotton.

Lines of machine stitching could also be used to make a traditional double outline of stitching around a quilting design. Doubling or echoing the line provides additional definition to the marks and pattern, adding to the visual effect of the piece, as seen on the North Country quilt on page 94.

Patterns of marks using continuous lines can be found in many stitched textiles. Japanese sashiko all-over stitch patterns based on the natural world are a good starting point for further exploration. There are some suggestions in the bibliography for finding out more.

Below: Sketchbook doodles in pen translated directly into continuous lines of machine stitch.

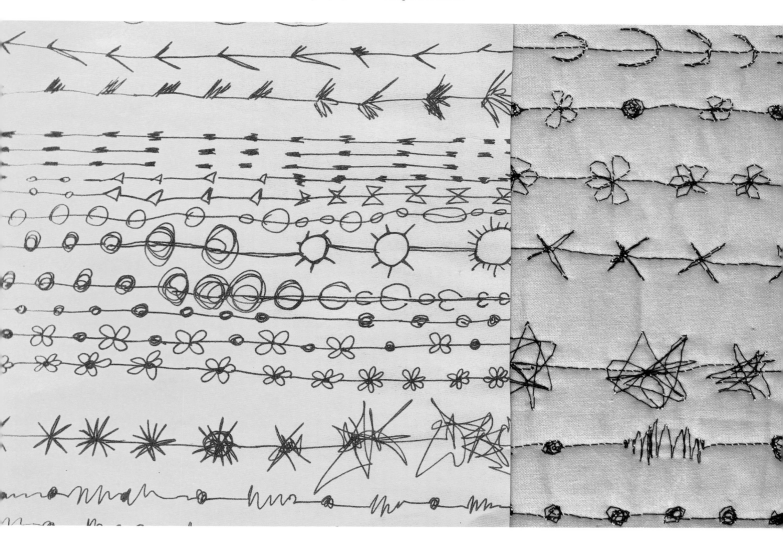

Dots, webs, and tufts

Webs and tufts can also be developed from single stitch marks. The illustration below shows a sequence of stitch marks in black and white; it was started with dots and then these were developed to create webs and tufts. The first dot was stitched and the needle lifted, the fabric was moved, and then another dot was stitched. The process was continued across the textile work. In the piece below right, there is an area of dots to the right where the connecting threads have been left in place as a triangular network. The sample also shows areas where the joining threads have been trimmed and retained as fine tufts around each dot. Both webs and tufts have been worked in white on black and in black on white to explore the differences between the stitch marks.

The illustration opposite of web stitch marks and tufts shows a richer and more subtle effect, achieved by working in purple and green threads on green cotton sateen. The tufts make a wispier and more subtle mark than the tails on the hand-tied reef knots seen earlier, because machine-sewing threads tend to be finer than hand-sewing threads.

Opposite: Machine-stitched webs and tufts on green cotton sateen.

Below: Dots, webs, and tufts machine-stitched in black rayon thread on white acrylic satin and white rayon thread on vintage black rayon fabric.

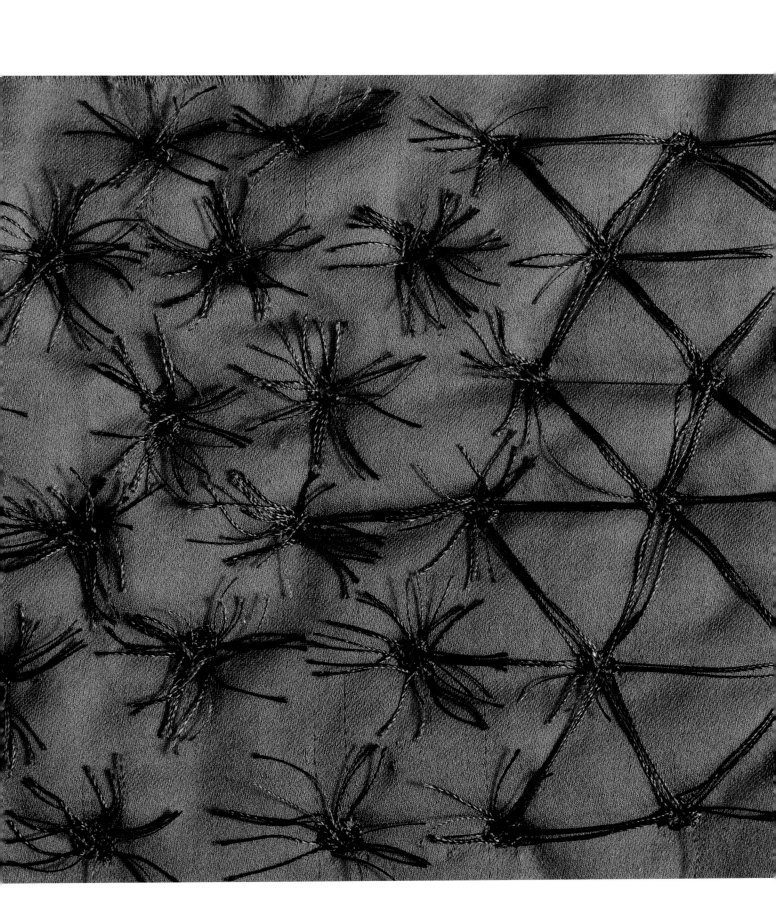

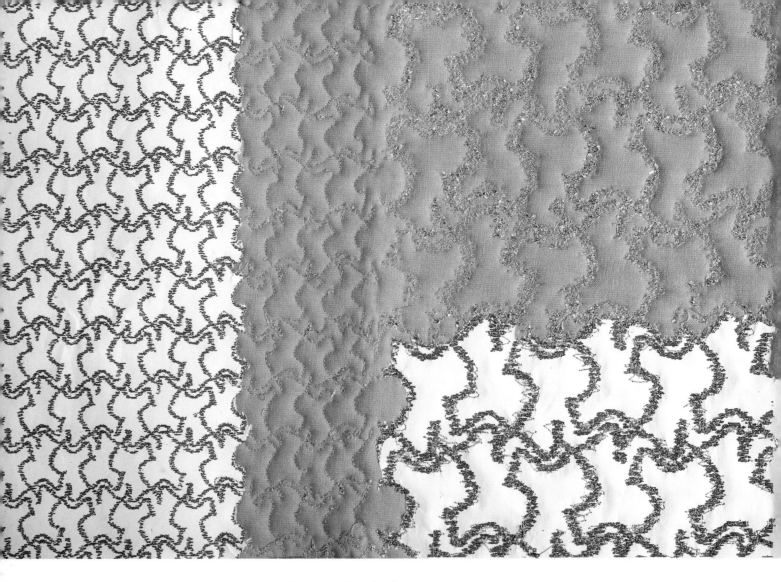

Layered stitch marks

Above: Abstract all-over pattern with free-machined stitch marks in two sizes. Photocopies of the pattern were pinned to the fabrics and the pattern was machine-stitched through the paper. The paper was then torn away.

Right: A grid of free machine-stitched marks worked in successive layers of colored threads to build up the design.

Machine-stitched marks can be built up in layers to create rich surfaces. The examples shown offer only two possibilities. The illustration above shows an abstract all-over pattern in two sizes. The pattern was taken from the tiny pattern found on the lining of an envelope. It was enlarged on a photocopier several times, and two sizes of copies were selected. These were then pinned to the fabrics and the pattern was machine-stitched through the paper. Once the basic pattern was clear on the fabric, the paper was torn away and further stitching was added to the large pattern to make bolder marks.

The sample on the right was machine-stitched in a sequence across a basic grid. The green fabric was marked with the small central squares and then layered with batting beneath. I started the machine stitching with a layer of white or green stitch around each small square. The square holes were then cut out and further stitches added, which were built up to cover the background fabric. Another layer of machine-stitched marks in variegated thread (blue/green/yellow) enhanced each square hole. A final layer of yellow marks was made to radiate outwards from each hole.

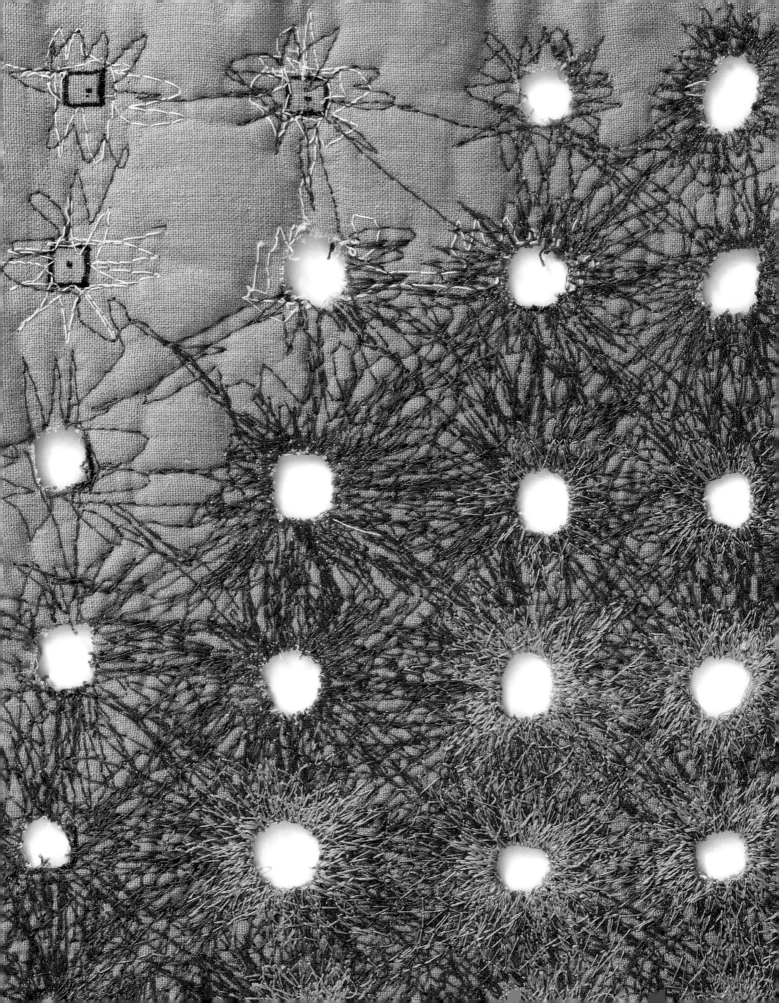

Working in threads and fabrics of the same color

Stitch marks can be developed using threads and fabrics of the same color, contrasting colors and many colors. In North Country quilting, the thread is usually the same color as the fabric and is stitched in small, regular marks. The result is subtle, with shadows and a pattern that is often only visible in a good light. The illustration below, a detail of an early twentieth-century North Country wholecloth quilt from the Quilters' Guild of the British Isles Collection, shows this beautiful effect. The quilt is shown in full on page 125.

Applying this traditional quilting practice of working with fabrics and threads of the same color to contemporary threads and fabrics can produce some interesting results. The circle pieces shown on the left were worked in self-color: cream on cream and black on black. They are part of a series of paired works exploring the idea of living together peacefully, titled *Harmonious Living*. This light and dark pair were made using the hand-worked spiral stitch explained on page 70. Both pairs were stitched in threads that matched the background fabrics closely in both color and fiber composition.

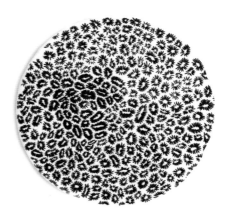

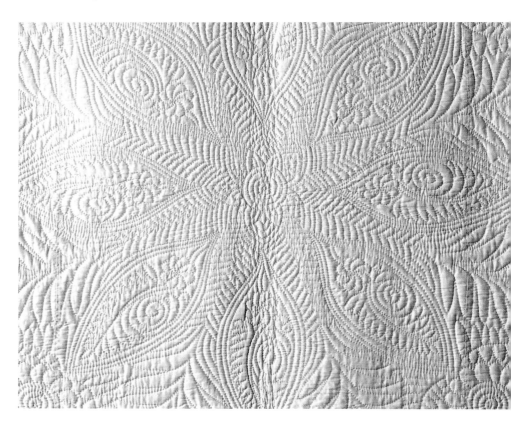

Harmonious Living series: two pairs from a set of sixteen pieces. From top: Spiral stitch cream on cream, spiral stitch black on black, coralline stitch black on white, coralline stitch white on black.

Above: Detail of early twentieth century North Country wholecloth quilt from the Collection of the Quilters' Guild of the British Isles. The whole quilt is shown on page 125.

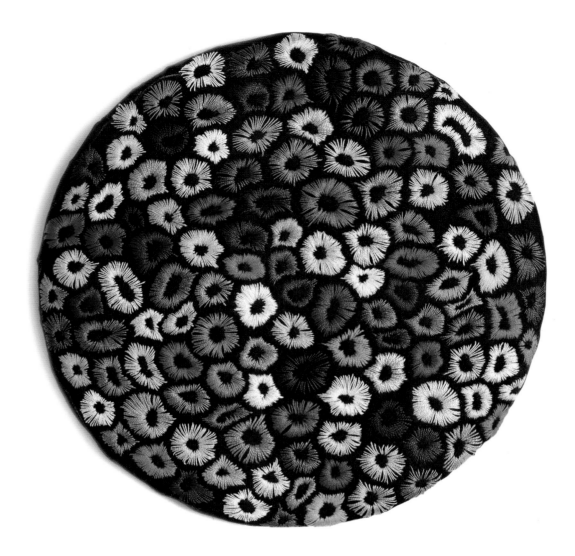

Using contrast and color in fabrics and threads

In the lower two pieces shown far left, the use of black thread on white fabric and vice versa makes the stitch marks highly visible. This contrast was strengthened further by a considered choice of thread. The white marks were made with a double thread of mercerized cotton with a slight sheen. The black marks were made with a slightly fluffy synthetic thread. The piece above used a random selection of colored cotton perle threads. The pieces are the same finished size and their entire surfaces are stitched, yet the results are quite different.

To my eye, the multicolored piece lacks some of the variability and subtlety seen in the black and white examples.

The use of threads that contrast strongly with the background fabric opens up bolder possibilities for stitch marks. The black and white webs and tufts seen on page 90 give a sense of the boldness possible when working with contrasting fabrics and threads. Try working with contrast to aid the exploration of new ideas for stitch marks, or to challenge your usual ways of working.

If you are interested in working further with stitch marks and contrast, it is worth exploring Japanese sashiko quilting (see suggestions in the Bibliography). Traditionally, sashiko patterns were worked in white thread on indigo fabrics. In the finest work, the individual stitches were very precisely placed and the contrast between the color of the fabric and the thread showed this precision and skill to advantage. Contemporary work reveals a wider range of color combinations.

It can be a worthwhile exercise to explore a specific stitch mark using the same color of fabric and thread, and then contrast and color. The round pieces shown opposite and above are of works made using a hand-stitched mark developed from the radiant stitch mark samples seen on page 68. I call this stitch mark 'coralline.'

6 Making it real

For many artists and makers, the early development stages of the creative process can be very enjoyable and often lead to many experimental paper works and textile samples. So far, so good; but how do these paper works and samples lead you to a finished art textile? In this section we will run through the key stages of the creative process, materials and equipment, and at the end of the chapter, a diagram and a series of images illustrate two ways of thinking about developing a finished piece.

Detail of hand stitching on *Circular Form* showing the variety of colors in the hand-dyed cotton thread. The full piece is shown on page 109.

Inspiration

Inspiration is key to making textile work. Any maker or artist needs ideas to explore, and the drive to make artwork from them. Landscape often provides a stimulus. The work of the English painters Constable, Turner, Cotman, and Nash was part of my visual education. I live in northern England and as you have seen from the images throughout this book, I continue to be inspired by the seasonal colors, marks, and the history and complexity of the landscapes around me.

My locality has been marked and changed by many things: human settlements, lead mining, quarrying, farming, road-making, and railway-building, amongst others. Subtle changes in vegetation during different seasons, or at times of drought or snowfall, can reveal something of the past. I am interested in the ways that people have interacted with the local geology over the centuries. The well-worn footpath, the stone wall around a field, and the carved rock have all been inspirational.

Above: Two pages from a sketchbook on color in the landscape.

Opposite: Sketchbook page from a daybook.

My deep visual awareness and knowledge develops from being in the landscape throughout the year, in most weathers. I have been inspired further by exploring these landscapes with different companions. Walking and talking with a geologist, engineer, painter, miner, or botanist can be both fascinating and frequently surprising.

In the *Shifting Sands* series of work illustrated throughout this book, I sought to express something of the inspiration and beauty I find in beaches, particularly those in Cornwall and Norfolk. Beaches in winter are often very different to the way that they appear in summer. The marks are bolder and the shapes are bigger as the winter storms rework and reshape the sand. Getting to know one beach really well over many years led to a long series of textiles exploring sand ripples, using hand-stitched marks.

Cold Pole Mill be felted — cut + inlaid to give 2 tone effect? +ve & -ve millstone ⊙ ⊙

lunar + seasonal

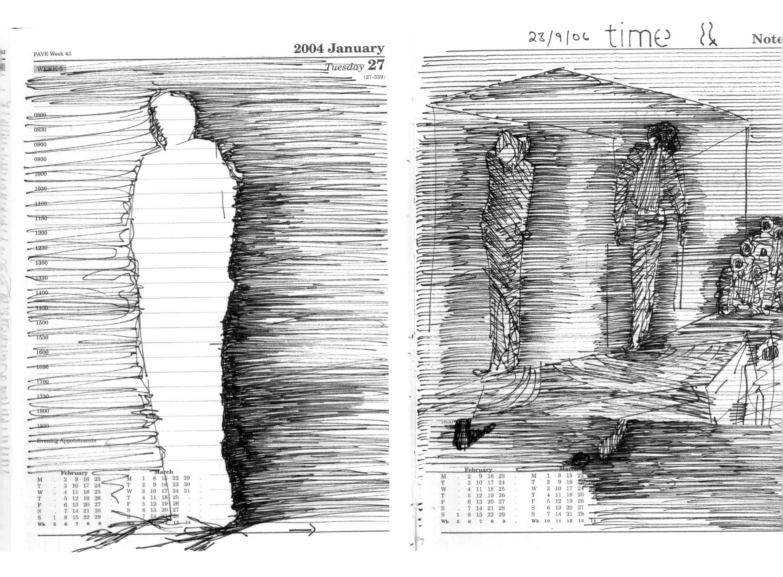

Two pages from
the sketchbooks of
Carolyn Curtis Magri.
Hand-drawn marks on
the pages of an out-
of-date diary.

Inspiration can also arise from more transient visual contact. Many of us enjoy opportunities to travel, to see and experience places, cultures, and landscapes beyond our own. We may only be able to visit distant places once in our lifetime, yet they can be so inspiring. Using this fleeting and potentially more superficial visual acquaintance as inspiration will be different to the experience of working with local sources. You can visit your local museum to see collections of historical, natural, and contemporary objects from many parts of the world to follow up inspiration and interests derived from distant places.

Using a sketchbook

Recording your travels, developing your ideas and keeping notes, planning a finished piece of artwork, or meeting the assessment requirements of a formal course can all be reasons for keeping and using a sketchbook. Sketchbooks can be full of beautifully painted and drawn pages; they can be vacation journals with quick sketches of views and people seen along the way, or project books; or they may be scrapbooks of cuttings and images, or even box files and suitcases as the need arises.

For many artists, sketchbooks are fundamental to their work and thinking. Their choices and working methods have evolved over time, with sustained thought and practice. The key to using a sketchbook is to explore what suits you, your ideas, context, and working methods. Books are available in a wide range of sizes and formats. For example, surveyors use durable, high-quality field notebooks made for outdoor use. The use of a surveyor's notebook as a project sketchbook may add meaning to the development of a series of textile works based on landscape or buildings. You may even like to make your own sketchbook as part of your creative process (it may become an artwork in its own right). See the Bibliography (page 127) for some starting points.

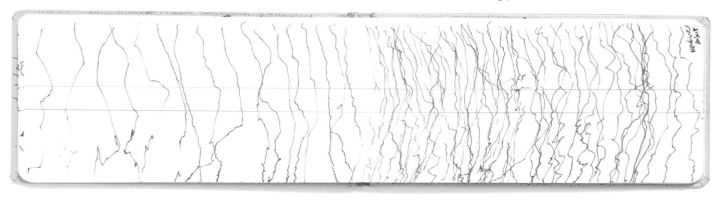

Surveyor's notebook used as a sketchbook for a project on traveling.

At exhibitions and end-of-year shows for art and textile courses, there are often wonderful sketchbooks developed as part of a student's formal course work requirements. For the rest of us, different and more sustainable practical approaches to sketchbook-keeping may be needed. Some examples of my sketchbooks are shown above and on pages 98, 99, 100, and 102. My current solution is to have several sketchbooks in use at any one time, each with a specific function:

- A letter-sized daybook or scrapbook containing handwritten notes, tickets, sketches, postcards, cuttings, photos, small stitched fragments, scribbles, doodles, long thoughts, quotes, random ideas, invitations, press releases, and so on. Gathering the materials and writing notes in the daybook keeps

Above: Two pages from a small sketchbook on the theme of marks.

Below, left to right: Felt pen, blue and white grease pencils, graphite pencils of varying densities, wax crayons, and a white wax candle.

items safe and my mind clear, because I know that these items and ideas are available if I want to refer to them.

- A small, softback, lightweight notebook for my handbag/rucksack/suitcase, for rapid notes and sketches with whatever pen or pencil comes to hand.
- Several themed sketchbooks developed over years as I continue to collect relevant materials and to explore specific ideas in sketches, drawings, and collages. Current themes include paths, circles, and grids.
- Specific project sketchbooks holding the 'workings out' of the project idea, drawings, proposals, calculations, plans, contact details, suppliers, costs, and so on. The project sketchbook supports the development and delivery of the whole project, not just the art aspects. Project books vary in size and format to respond to the project in hand.

Artist Carolyn Curtis Magri used blank and out-of-date diaries as sketchbooks for a long series of drawings called *Screamers*, on the theme of prisons. Two of these images are shown on page 100. This sketchbook-based practice enabled the artist to refine her ideas and images so that when she did have time in the studio to paint, the work flowed more easily.

Choosing a focus

Below, top left to bottom right: pencils, craft knife, dye palettes, brush, and mixing palette.

When you start working through the creative possibilities open to you, there is likely to be an overwhelming range of options to choose from. This range can be made more approachable and manageable in various ways. You could choose to focus on one theme, or one technique, or even one stitch mark. Using a narrow focus for a period of time allows you to explore something more fully, to simplify your ideas and options by reducing the distractions.

Alternatively, it can be liberating to decide that for the next year (or however long you choose), you will not make any finished work for exhibition or to commission and then to spend the time exploring and developing your own ideas. Another way of making creative work more manageable is to choose to make work for a deadline, say an exhibition a year or two ahead. Clear decisions such as these can feel unduly restrictive at first; however, they can be very helpful in supporting the development of your personal creative voice and the choice is not for ever, after all.

At one point, I decided to work solely with hand-made running-stitch marks for the next year. At the end of the year, I reviewed my progress. Gradually, my focus on the hand-stitched mark led me to an exploration of the marks made by looped threads and then to exploring the marks made by tying knots. The work arising from this choice of focus is the basis of this book.

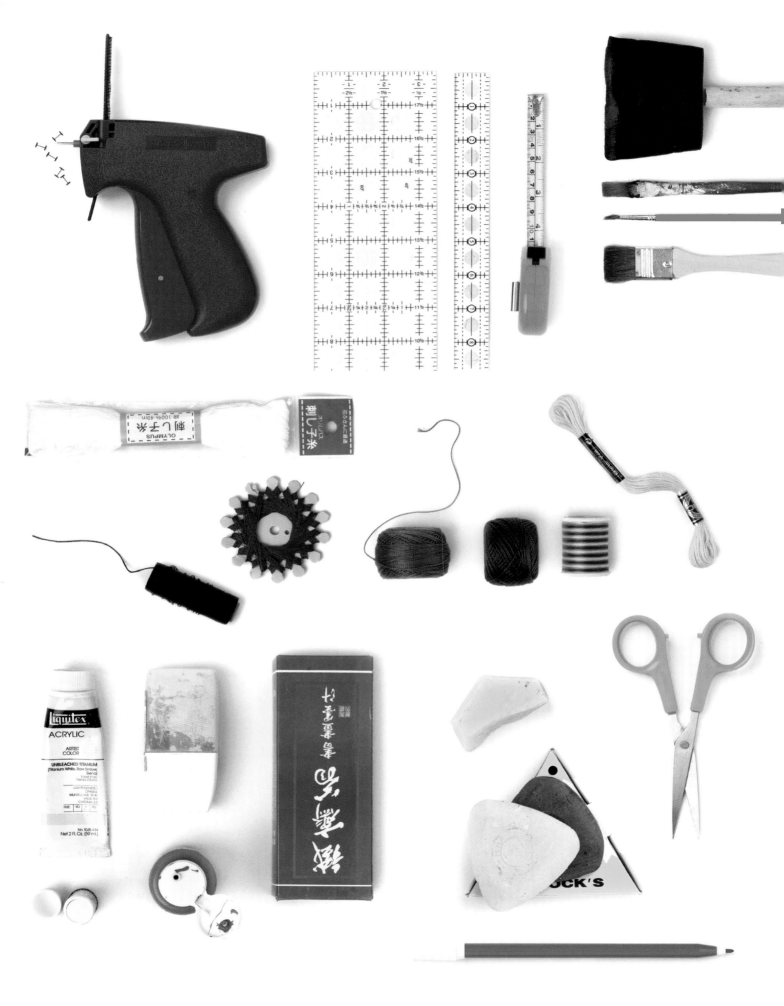

Materials and equipment

When you are making textile work, there is a vast array of materials and equipment available to you. Where do you begin? What do you really need? What would suit you? Do ask advice from friends, look at what other people use, and consider attending a day workshop that will guide you through experiments with products and their possibilities. Such workshops can be great fun and are a chance to meet like-minded people. Practicing under expert guidance can open up unexpected insights into materials and ways of approaching your themes.

Thinking carefully about the equipment and materials that may suit you, your ideas, and your working space is time well spent. It is important to use fabrics and media that you enjoy working with and can use safely. I generally prefer working with natural fibers to working with synthetic materials. I often use cotton calico, a robust fabric with a slight texture that adds an extra layer of subtle marks to the work. It often takes me a year or more to make a piece of textile work. Therefore it is important that I am comfortable while working and that I enjoy the process, especially the stitching, which often takes the greatest part of the making time.

The work within this book has been created using a range of materials and equipment (see the illustrations on pages 102–104 and 120–121). This has been gathered over the years from a variety of places, including charity shops and jumble sales, swaps with friends, my travels, and buying from specialist suppliers.

Threads and fabrics

It is very useful to have a stock of materials, threads, and fabrics to draw on, and it is tempting and enjoyable to collect as wide a range of materials as possible. As your work develops, it may be worth looking around DIY and hardware stores for threads and materials outside your usual range.

If your budget and storage space are limited, necessity is the mother of invention, as the proverb says. Improvise by using a different type of paper, thread, or fabric to your original plan. This can lead to happy accidents: the new item can behave differently, adding an additional element to the work. For example, red shirring elastic can be substituted for red cotton thread, with interesting and lively results. Experimentation is important and such discoveries can take the maker in new directions.

Alternatively, it is helpful to be able to create your own materials on a small scale. Papers are easily painted to match an idea, and fabrics can be colored using paints or pens. Do check the manufacturer's instructions for information on the colorfastness and durability of the product if the work may be sold or is likely to be washed.

One aspect of working with stitched marks is the challenge of finding threads that exactly suit the marks being made. From time to time it may be impossible to find thread of a specific type, color, or mix of colors. Try using diluted artists' acrylic paint, fiber-reactive dyes, or silk paints to color small quantities of cotton and linen hand-sewing threads. The finish on hand-colored threads can

Opposite, top row: Quilters' tacking gun with tacks, gridded quilting rulers, tape measure, foam brush, different-sized brushes.
Middle: selection of hand and machine sewing threads including white sashiko thread.
Bottom row: artists's acrylic paints and household paint, calligraphy ink, beeswax block, dressmakers' chalk in gray and white, small sharp scissors, blue washable marker pen.

Above: Cotton reel label.

In choosing materials for making a piece of textile work I always ask myself 'What am I trying to express?', before considering which materials will best support my ideas. As you continue to practice and make personal textile work, it will become easier for you to answer this question and make appropriate choices of materials.

be quite variable and may be well suited to natural subjects. With practice and preparation, it is possible to obtain very even finishes. If you draw hand-colored thread through a block of beeswax before stitching, it contributes to a more even finish and makes sewing smoother. Keep a sample of the threads made and a record of the colors used, in case you wish to repeat the process. The French knots shown on page 78 were made with a white thread colored with diluted yellow artists' acrylic paint, and the threads used in *Circular Form* on page 109 were colored with fiber-reactive dyes.

Sampling

It can take months, or longer, to make a stitched textile piece, so it is essential to be sure that the outcome will meet your original vision. The making of samples allows ideas to be tested inexpensively and quickly, using small quantities of different fabrics and threads, before making final choices. Try out several fabric and thread combinations to find what works best. Sometimes the 'right' combination of mark, technique, and materials comes quickly: the answer just pops into your head or appears beneath your fingers. At other times, the originating idea can be very strong, but nothing seems to be right when you are

Pink baby quilt made from a traditional North Country wholecloth design showing a corner and butted edges.

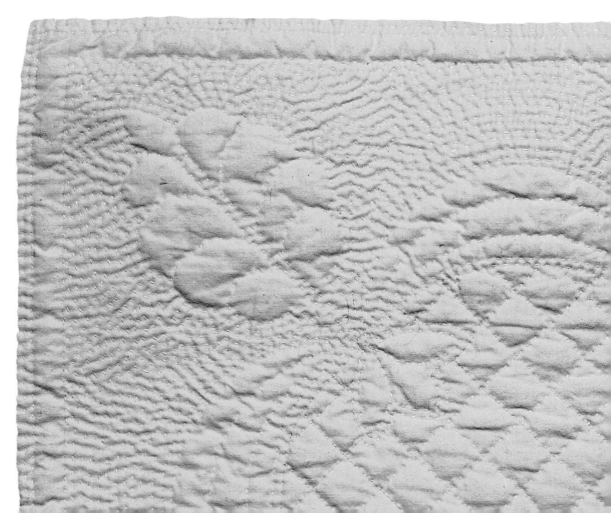

Above: *Red Radiant*: detail of hand-stitched marks.

making stitched mark samples to develop it. This can be frustrating when you want to make progress with an idea. However, it is often a good opportunity to explore beyond your usual vocabulary of marks, techniques, and materials and to reach for something new. Some options to try are:

- Using different fabric colors and types.
- Changing the backing fabric.
- Adding or changing the batting layer.
- Using a different size of needle.
- Making hand-sewn marks rather than machined ones, or vice versa.
- Using a different type or thickness of thread.
- Stitching with the grain of the fabric or against it.
- Stitching on the bias.

Often, the right stitch mark will be the one that feels most exciting to you.

Reference collection

Gradually, paper works/designs and textile samples will accumulate, potentially 'silting up' parts of your working space. Together they form a valuable record of work made, ideas considered, and problems solved, and they can be retained indefinitely if space permits. However, it may be preferable to edit what you keep and retain only the key stitched textile samples for your reference collection and dispose of the rest. You can refer to the collection when an idea or technique is to be reused, or for problem-solving when making new work. If kept out of the light, textile samples will last and continue to inspire you for many years.

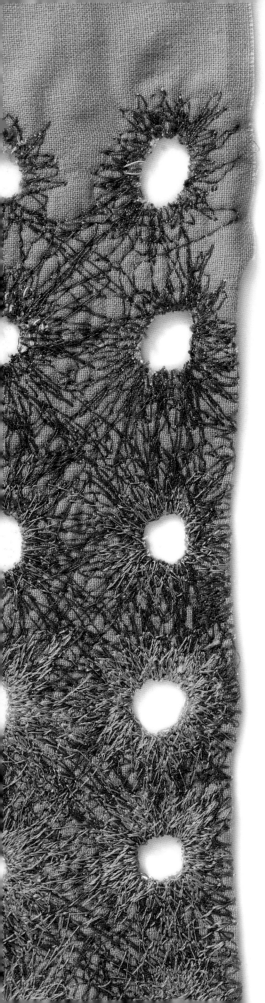

Finishing

Ideally, the edges and finish of a textile artwork should integrate with the idea and the purpose of the piece, adding to its impact and not distracting from it. Consider the finishing and edges when planning the work, as it is likely to minimize the work needed. Textile work that is likely to be washed, such as a bed quilt, will need suitably durable and practical edges. Work made primarily for display still needs finishing to withstand subsequent handling. There are many options for edges. A suggestion using densely worked machine stitch is shown left; there are a couple of further suggestions below.

The butted edges found in traditional North Country quilts make a neat and durable edge. The use of a traditional edging treatment is particularly appropriate for works that draw inspiration from textile history. Butted edges are made by neatly folding the accurately trimmed top and bottom edges of the quilt under and together, with the raw edges to the inside. The folded edges are matched and then stitched together by hand, or by machine, as shown on page 106. Corners can be mitred to form a square, or they can be rounded a little.

Some textile work is best finished by being stretched over a frame, such as a wooden stretcher, and then stapled to hold it taut, trimming and tucking in any raw edges as you work to ensure a smooth finish. This often suits smaller stitched pieces, which can lack presence without a frame of some kind. Stretchers can be bought in different shapes, sizes and depths from art shops and sometimes from discount shops. The *Harmonious Living* pieces on page 94 were mounted on a set of circular stretchers. The long stretcher used for the buttercups piece on page 73 was custom-made.

Case study: *Circular Form*

This textile piece has its origins in an inspirational visit to Australia. I wanted to work with my memories of our travels and to make a personal (not for exhibition) piece to suit our house. My experiences of traveling to very different parts of the world can take years to 'settle' and become integrated into my visual awareness and language. This time I wanted to make a textile piece quickly, before my memories were smoothed by the passage of time. I have often photographed circular forms and worked with imagery of circles, so it was a familiar form. The piece also marked a return to working in my studio, a personal version of coming full circle and arriving back where you started.

I had distinct ideas about some aspects of the piece. From my Australian images and memories I knew I wanted a sense of slender, chalky marks made by hand, maybe using both hand stitch and paint to give the feel of handwritten marks. I envisaged the work in pale, earthy colors on a dark ground, probably with some quilting to give texture and stability to the finished piece. I wanted to use some brown linen recycled from a worn-out dress that held good memories. The size of the finished work was dictated by the size of the linen pieces.

I have set out in words the creative process I used to make the finished piece on pages 110 and 111, in words at the top of the page and visually below. One of these ways of working and thinking may resonate with you more strongly than

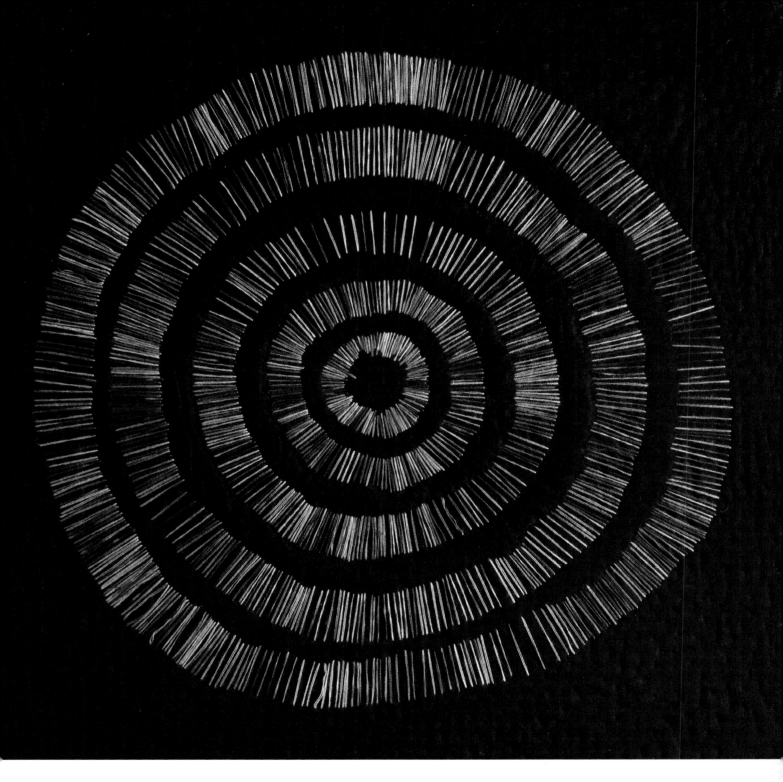

Above: *Circular Form,* 23½in x 23½in (60cm x 60 cm).

Opposite: Sample edge: the bottom area is complete, while the top area is not yet tucked under and stitched.

the other, or you may prefer to use both together. It is worth reflecting on your preferred ways of working and how you could apply this insight to developing your work. The completed piece is above and a detail of the stitch marks is on page 97.

Case study: *Circular Form* creative process as a diagram with words

1. Collecting and choosing source images of my Australian visit.

2. Drawing a mind-map-type diagram of ideas to clear my mind.

3. A series of experiments exploring the type of mark to use, their scale and their layout, working mostly on paper, using some of the techniques covered previously:
   - Pencil and colored pencil drawings.
   - Working with wax crayon resists, oil pastels, and brown ink.
   - Cutting slashes in painted papers folded into curves to mimic long, colored stitches.
   - Doodling on linen scraps with acrylic paints using dots and lines.

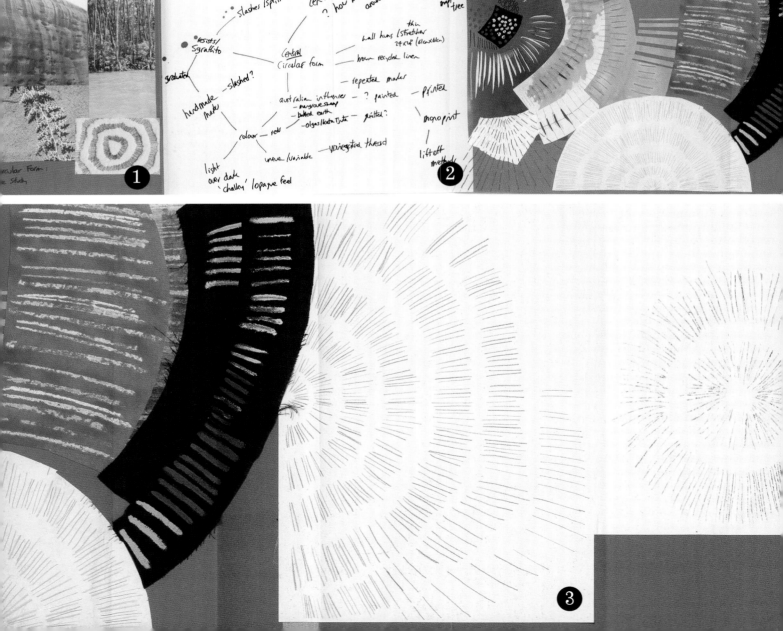

4. This initial phase enabled me to see that resists would be a good way to develop the idea further, because the resist marks gave a raised effect akin to hand stitch. More resist drawings to explore and decide possible layouts.

5. Making stitch samples:
   - Replicating the raised marks by hand-stitching long marks on to a single top layer of linen and batting. (The lack of a backing layer made the stitches more raised. The piece was intended for display on a wooden stretcher so the reverse was not important.)
   - Trying different threads and stitches (couching, straight stitch).

6. Tried a variegated pale perle thread: too pale and too thick! The thread chosen was a twin-stranded mercerized cotton sourced from a jumble sale, then partially dyed using different colors of fiber-reactive dyes with salt and soda solutions.

7. The resulting ball of unevenly variegated and slightly sheeny cotton thread turned out to be exactly right for making this piece of work. Stitching – regular reviews of work in progress to check layout and effect. All colored stitching completed.

8. Working directly on the textile only now, checked work for final effect and decided that the plain areas and edges needed to be treated in some way so that the piece looked finished: decided to use small, all-over stitch marks in a matching dark brown thread for subtlety.

9. Stretched stitched textile taut on a wooden stretcher using a staple gun.

Creative process diagram showing the development process of making *Circular Form*, shown on page 109.

7 Living a creative life

Creative strategies

Certain strategies will support your creative journey as your ideas evolve, events occur and your circumstances change. Sometimes it is easy to find the time and energy for a creative life and making textile artworks: the ideas flow, the work is completed, and the opportunities to share and exhibit arrive without apparent effort. At other times it can be real struggle to make anything at all, and the practical limitations of time and space seem too overwhelming for any satisfying creative results to be possible. There are many interrelated aspects to living a creative life, and I consider some on pages 114–119.

Harmonious Living series: two pairs of light and dark hand-stitched pieces from a set of eight pairs.

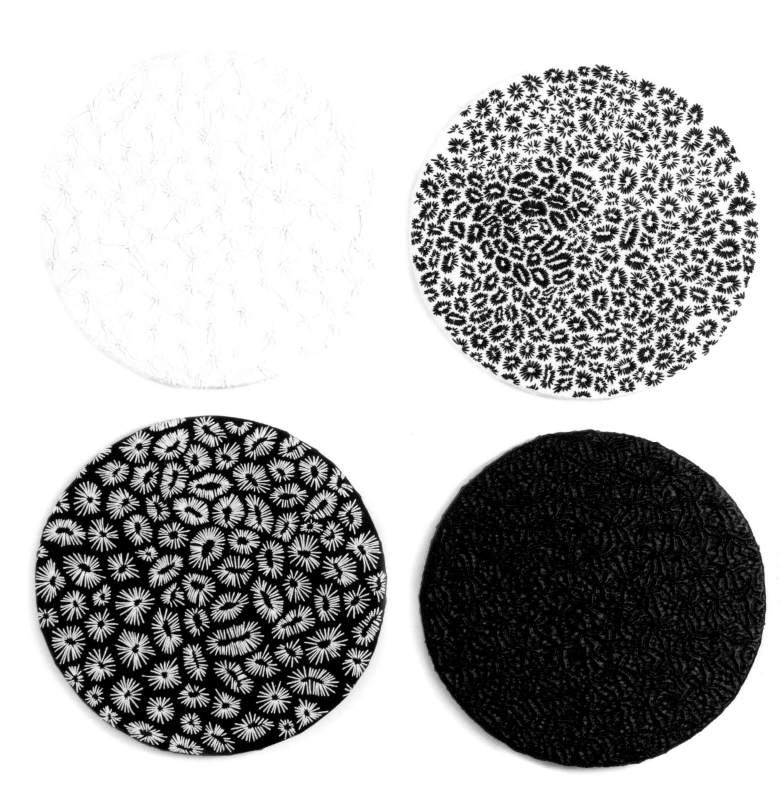

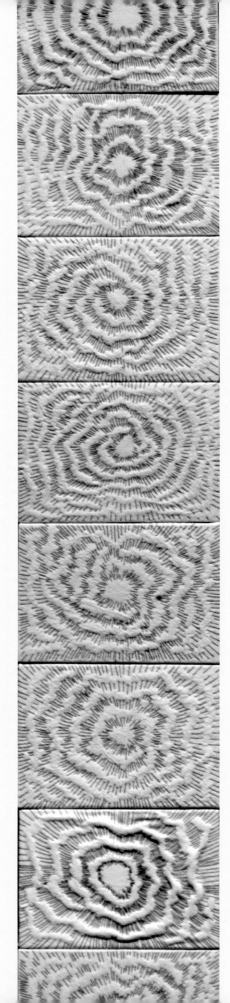

Health and safety

It is very important to take care of yourself and those who share your workspace. The joy of making textile art is the ongoing excitement and possibilities that this vast field offers over a lifetime. There is always another idea, technique, or collection to explore. However, ignoring your own well-being can impair your enjoyment and creative potential. Although sewing and art are generally seen as easy, relaxing, and relatively safe activities, there are still aspects of health and safety to take into account.

It is important to work where you have sufficient space to move around safely, with suitable lighting (would a daylight bulb be helpful?) and adequate ventilation for the activity if required. Always wear the appropriate protective equipment and clothing. When using paints and other specialist media, do read and act on the manufacturer's instructions for safe usage. Dyes, in particular, can be harmful if not used correctly.

When carrying out any activity, it is important to think about your posture and the way that you are using your body. For example, when sewing or drawing, are you sitting comfortably and are you able to work without strain on any part of your body? When using your sewing machine, is your seat at the right height for the machine bed and table? How can you best support the size and weight of the textile piece you are working on? Do you need to make any adjustments if the piece you are working on is especially large or heavy? Are you taking enough breaks from repetitive activities and stretching your body? Regular breaks give the mind and body a chance to relax.

We are all different, and it may take some time to get the details right. This section is intended to prompt you to consider what you really need and to ensure that when you are working creatively, it is comfortable and sustainable for you.

Motivation

Why do we make textile art? From a personal perspective, I see being creative as a fundamental human drive. To me, a life without making things would not be worth living. Of course, I create and maintain many things in daily life that are important to me and that I generally don't consider to be

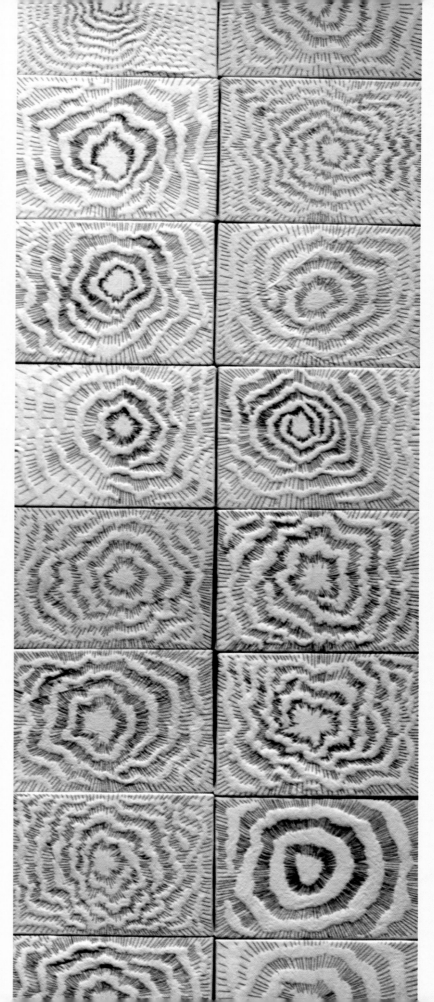

Left and opposite:
Radiant Miniatures.
Each individual
piece is 7in x 5in
(18cm x 12cm).

art, including meals, the garden, and friendships. I also choose to make objects that I consider to be artworks. Making and exhibiting these objects provides me with a personal space to reflect, comment, express, and share my ideas. I have found that it is very useful and motivational to be clear about the importance that making art textiles plays in my life.

Traditional textiles and quilts were often made for weddings and other special family or community occasions, including fundraising for groups. Such social motivators are still important. A personal commitment to an exhibition or competition deadline, or membership of an active group of like-minded people who run workshops, exhibitions, and events can be valuable motivators for some people.

Another motivation may be the desire to express something about world events, politics, or social change. This may manifest as a one-off textile piece or become the basis of an artist's work for many years. In my own work, it was some years before I was moved to make any work directly influenced by external events. In 2005 world news seemed to become gloomier, and much of it seemed to relate to how difficult we find it to live harmoniously

Images arising from using time well. Photograph of Leverburgh harbor ramp taken while on vacation in the Hebrides (above); autumn color seen on my way to work (opposite page).

with people who appear to be different to ourselves. I explored this through making a composite textile piece entitled *Harmonious Living*, comprising sixteen paired, hand-stitched pieces. Each pair of pieces explored light and dark versions of the same stitch marks. Four of the group are shown on page 113.

Again, it can be helpful to consider why you make textiles. Understanding your own motivation can help you choose more easily between different activities and creative opportunities as they arise.

Time

Time is a key influence on textile work. Some historic textiles look like they have taken months or even years to stitch. We often seem to value textile work that explicitly shows that much time has been involved in its making, possibly through the presence of many small, perfect stitches or the vast scale of the work.

The time spent making can be valued as enjoyable; it is often meditative and sometimes healing. It allows for reflection and contemplation, which can lead to new ideas and new perspectives. Vacations may also offer time for reflection, seeing exhibitions,

developing ideas and making new work. Time is often a scarce resource, and using the time you have well is key to a creative life.

The passage of time can provide a chance to look back at the work you, or someone else, has made with different eyes. A review can provide new insight, as you bring greater life experience and visual experience when you see the work anew. Sometimes, work that did not appeal to you on initial acquaintance will make sense to you on later re-engagement. Reviewing familiar work over time can deepen your understanding of it. I noticed at a recent exhibition that North Country wholecloth hand quilting still resonates with me as strongly now as it did when I first saw it in the late 1980s.

Workspace

The available working environment affects the work you make. The processes that involve wet media such as paints or dyes can only be carried out in suitable spaces at home or in the studio. Other parts of the creative process, such as using sketchbooks, carrying out small-scale stitching, or computer-based activities can be done almost anywhere. The two images by

Carolyn Curtis Magri shown on page 100 were made during train journeys as a commuter. The work shown on pages 114 and 115, *Radiant Miniatures*, is a series of postcard-sized pieces I stitched whilst working and traveling away from home. Their small scale made it easy to make many pieces and enabled me to explore more of the possibilities of radiant stitch relatively quickly. The finishing and mounting of the work on individual wooden stretchers was done in my studio.

Having a dedicated workspace, either at home or in a studio building elsewhere, may be an unattainable ideal. Instead, make the most of the space you have by making sure that the materials you need are close at hand and easy to refer to.

Groups

Membership of a group can be invaluable. If you can't find a group, why not set one up? The Internet offers opportunities to join or create networks, and to create blogs. There is much to share with and learn from others, who may have found solutions that are of relevance to you. For example, housebound artists can contribute to postal or online exhibitions or resources.

Many artists now participate in open studios, held at their homes or at group studios. These offer valuable opportunities to see, buy, and discuss art directly with the maker. If you are thinking about renting a studio space in a group studio, attend their open studio (if they hold one). See page 126 for some starting points regarding places to visit.

Keeping your work moving

Sometimes, however motivated and committed you are, there are times when you will feel stuck. These times can be quite short in duration, although sometimes they can last for months or longer. You may be stuck on a practical or technical issue, or on a deeper challenge. The suggestions below have been helpful to me and others in keeping our creative work moving. Some of the suggestions will probably be ones you already use and some may not suit your working style; others may work once and some may open up new horizons. Do experiment and find out what works for you.
- Go for a walk.
- Take a break for tea or coffee, sitting outside if possible.
- Go to an exhibition: sometimes

the solution to a technical issue can be found by looking at how other people have solved similar problems.

- Go and see a film at the cinema. Notice how the film is constructed and filmed as a series of really large-scale visual images. How is color used? How are textiles used?
- Consult the members of any groups you belong to.
- Visit a museum: any type can yield useful ideas for textile work. Science and industrial museums can be surprisingly fruitful sources of imagery and technical information. Seeing objects in a wide range of materials, at large and small scales, and noticing the practical solutions used by others, can be very helpful in resolving problems with edges, colors, arranging space, or deciding how to fasten two materials together.
- Look at artwork in another medium e.g. painting, sculpture, video games, tapestry.
- Quilts and Australian Aboriginal paintings are sometimes made communally; does this way of working appeal to you?
- British North Country quilts and Australian Aboriginal paintings

are sometimes worked on from all sides and angles rather than from a single point. What would happen if you turned your work round and worked on it from the left or right side? Or worked from the center outwards, or from all sides? Or worked the piece as a double-sided piece?

- Look at other artists' statements and CVs for ideas on how they moved their work and careers forward.
- Go to the library and browse in the oversized picture books section.
- Enjoy the process of dyeing or painting some thread, paper, or fabric using whatever dyes or paints are readily to hand and without having any end uses in mind.
- Go swimming or participate in some other form of exercise.
- Invite a friend round to discuss and possibly help to resolve the problem.
- Look at your reference collection of samples and see what still inspires you.

Keeping your work moving. Two images from rural and urban walks: countryside in Derbyshire (top), the remains of a burnt tire (above).

If the feeling of being stuck seems to be long-lasting and resistant to change, here are some further suggestions for ways to approach the situation.

- Do something creative every day, however small it is.
- Try another creative activity such as gardening, baking, talking, or writing.
- Go out: the solution may be out there. For practical and visual solutions, museums work best for me. For example, I found the solution to a long-standing issue of how to finish a quilt edge by seeing how a cabinet-maker had finished some drawer joints.
- Talk to someone from another arts discipline—such as a writer, poet or architect—about how he or she works and keeps work moving forwards.
- Attend a public lecture, or talk to someone working in a scientific discipline such as technology or engineering, and find out how he or she works and solves problems.
- Assess other arts disciplines for any useful parallels with your own practice. Taking literature as an example, consider what you are trying to do: are you trying to write an essay, a short story, a novel, or a film script?

If you want to explore creativity further, two books by Julia Cameron (see Bibliography, page 127) are fascinating reading.

Days out

The development of your personal textile work is likely to be enhanced by developing your knowledge of visual imagery in parallel. A day out looking at the creative work of others can be very inspiring and clarifying. Galleries and museums offer great learning possibilities. Exhibitions focused on the work of a single artist or maker reveal that person's work in some depth, showing you how he or she works, and ideas and concerns. Graduation shows are often fascinating to visit.

It can be very valuable to make visits in the company of others, and to explore what they see and how it differs from what you see, and thus enrich your experience and understanding.

Days out: detail of a street in Hull's Fruitmarket area.

8 Resources

The following are suggestions for materials and equipment which you will find useful as you develop your design and textile work.

Materials

Paints
- Watercolor, Brusho, metallic paints, ready-mixed poster paints, gouache, acrylics, fabric paints, household paints.

Pencils/crayons
- Wax crayons, candles, grease pencils (a white grease pencil is most useful; other colors are available), watercolor pencils, graphite pencils of different hardness, oil pastels, water-soluble crayons such as Neocolor.

Pens/inks
- Felt-tip pens of many types, ballpoint pens, fiber-tip pens, calligraphy pens and inks, ink pen and a range of nibs, fountain pen inks.

Dyes
- Fiber-reactive dyes e.g. Dylon, silk paints.

Paper
- Heavyweight lining paper (sold for wallpapering), tissue paper, tracing paper, cartridge paper, graph paper, and squared paper. Layout paper for working on designs: it is useful to have large pads. Papers made from a range of fibers (banana, jute, hemp, bamboo, and so on), textured watercolor paper, brown and colored wrapping papers, recycled paper, envelopes, light card, plastics, and corrugated cardboard from packaging.

Glue
- Glue stick and PVA glue for thick or heavy works.

Fabric and thread
- Natural-fiber fabrics and threads, including calico and muslin. New and recycled cotton fabrics, including sheeting, calico, silk, and linen.
- Batting: 2oz (50g) polyester batting, cotton batting, woolen blankets.
- Threads: machine-sewing threads, flower threads, upholstery-weight threads, crochet yarns, and specialist quilting threads in a range of thicknesses and fibers including cotton, linen, silk, rayon, and polyester. Beeswax block for smoothing threads before sewing.

Printing
- Artists' acrylic paints and water-based oil colors in tubes. Cardboard and styrofoam to make printing blocks. Carbon papers sold for copying.

Miscellaneous
- Useful items include, but are not limited to: sticky tape, masking tape, florists' wire, newspaper, magazines, pipe cleaners, sticks and twigs, string, twine, raffia, elastic bands, old ballpoint pens, coffee stirrers, cotton buds, feathers, rags, sponges.

Equipment

Printing

- Small pieces of perspex or wood to use as a printing surface.
- Hand rollers or a wooden spoon to rub the back of a printed image to ensure that it transfers evenly.
- Old towels or padding for the printing table.
- A hand-operated printing press (optional). If you know you will want to print a great deal of paper and fabric, a printing press is lovely to have. Printing presses can also be accessed through group studios, usually for a fee.

Sewing

- Hand-sewing needles in a range of sizes.
- Machine needles in a range of sizes for fabrics of different types.
- Long glass-headed pins, flower pins, and curved safety pins.
- Sewing machine with feed dogs that can be dropped to allow free machining; manufacturer's instruction book.
- Steam iron and an adjustable-height ironing board.
- Stitch ripper.

Measuring and cutting

- Scissors, ideally several pairs: a sharp pair used only for fabrics, a small, pointed pair for fine work, and a pair for cutting paper. Pinking shears and other specialist scissors are sometimes useful. Buy scissors that feel comfortable to use.
- Metal yardstick.

- 12in (30cm) plastic ruler and a specialist gridded quilting ruler.
- Tape measures in fabric and metal, preferably retractable, including an 118in (3m) one for large work and for hanging exhibitions.
- Craft knife or scalpel with spare blades.
- Stanley knife with retractable blade.
- Self-healing cutting mat, in as large a size as you can find space for.
- Awl or stiletto for punching holes.
- Craft punches for making specific shapes.
- Templates, either bought or home-made.
- L-shaped card frames or masks in a range of colors.
- Domestic wood saw or hacksaw for cutting battens or other items to size.

For working with art media

- Various brushes and other means of applying paint in a wide range of sizes and types: foam brushes for laying down large areas of color, household decorating brushes, small brushes, calligraphy brushes, spatulas.

Computing, design, and photography

- Computer and relevant software.
- Color printer and scanner or photocopier (can be combined in a single machine).
- Digital camera, possibly the camera on your mobile phone.
- Papers for printing photographs.

Other useful equipment

- Plastic palettes or plastic food packaging.
- Yogurt pots, jam and coffee jars, plastic freezer boxes with lids.
- Hand-held magnifying lenses.
- Hammer and drill for mounting and finishing work as needed.
- Bone folder for making sharp creases in paper.
- Staple gun (hand or electric) for mounting work on stretchers.
- Quilters' tacking gun.

Suppliers

Dick Blick Art Materials
(800) 828-4548
www.dickblick.com
art supplies, transfer papers

Utrecht Art Supply
(800)-223-9132
www. www.utrechtart.com
paints, papers, art supplies

PRO Chemical and Dye
(800) 228-9393
www.prochemicalanddye.com
fabrics, dyes, resists, textile art supplies

JoAnn Fabrics
www.joann.com
fabrics, threads, needles, batting,
sewing supplies

DMC
973-589-0606
www.dmc-usa.com
thread, needles, sewing and
embroidery notions

Organizations

AN, formerly Artists' Newsletter
www.a-n.co.uk

The Art House
www.the-arthouse.org.uk

Axis
www.axisweb.org

Embroiderers' Guild
www.embroiderersguild.com

Peak District Mines Historical Society
www.pdmhs.com

Quilt Art
www.quiltart.eu

Quilters' Guild
www.quiltersguild.org.uk

Yorkshire Artspace Society
www.artspace.org.uk/

Path series, 5in x 35in x 1½in (13cm x
89cm x 4cm). Calico and linen thread.

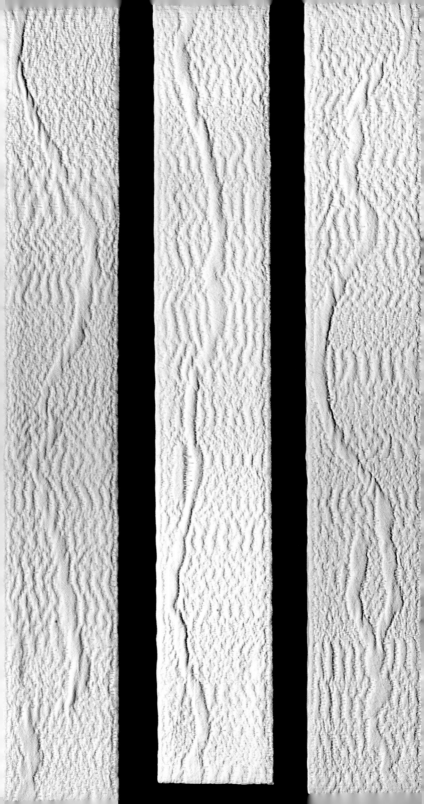

Acknowledgements

A creative life ... with thanks to ...

This book has been many years and many journeys in the making. Countless friends, diverse colleagues, and students of all ages have contributed generously to the shaping of my ideas and work. Some of these contributions have been made in formal ways and some have been deeply practical; at other times, a passing comment has resonated and been amalgamated into my creative process.

I would like to make particular mention of the importance of groups in developing and sustaining my creative life. First it was the Pennine Quilters in Sheffield, then the European group, Quilt Art and the studio group, Yorkshire Artspace Society; more recently the Quilt Makers' Support Group, based in Sheffield, and the Contemporary Quilt Group of the Quilters' Guild of the British Isles have come to the fore. All of these groups have been invaluable sources of hospitality, support, information, and friendship. Being a member has provided the deadlines, the incentives, and the laughter that have enabled me and my work to keep moving on. Other members have refreshed my spirit and honed my intention through the highs and the lows of life. Whatever the form of your contributions, you have my grateful appreciation: it would not have been the same without you. This book is my synthesis of these experiences, shared knowledge and generosity. The content is, of course, an expression of my own views and experiences, and my responsibility.

This book is dedicated to those who were there at the beginning and those who fanned the early creative sparks. In particular, this book is for my parents, who could never have guessed where an early liking for 'making things' would lead. Much love and many thanks are also due to my husband Malcolm, for his many roles in bringing this book to completion. His support, patience, presence, and proofreading in particular have been invaluable.

I look forward to many more years of creative traveling with you all.

Opposite: Early twentieth-century North Country wholecloth quilt from the collection of the Quilters' Guild of the British Isles. A detail is shown on page 94.

Helen Parrott
Sheffield
2013

Bibliography

My wider life is reflected in my writing and in some of the references below.

Allen, Jeanne (1988). *Designer's Guide to Japanese Patterns*. Thames & Hudson.

Allen, Jeanne (1988). *Designer's Guide to Japanese Patterns 2*. Chronicle Books.

Briscoe, Susan (2005). *The Ultimate Sashiko Sourcebook*. David and Charles.

Box, Richard (1988). *Drawing and Design for Embroidery*. Batsford.

Butler, Anne (1983). *The Batsford Encyclopedia of Embroidery Stitches*. Batsford.

Buzan, Tony (2009). *The Mind Map Book*. BBC Books.

Campbell-Harding, Val and Pamela Watts (1989). *Machine Embroidery Stitch Techniques*. Batsford.

Cameron, Julia (1995). *The Artist's Way*. Pan Books.

Cameron, Julia (1996). *The Vein of Gold*. Pan Books.

Cooper, J. C. (1992) *An Illustrated Encyclopedia of Traditional Symbols*. Thames & Hudson.

Davidson, George (ed.) (2002). *Roget's Thesaurus*. Penguin.

Dean, Jenny (1999). *Wild Colour*. Mitchell Beazley.

Edwards, Betty (1982). *Drawing on the Right Side of the Brain*. Fontana.

Edwards, Betty (1992). *Drawing on the Artist Within*. Fontana.

Ford, T. D. and J. H. Rieuwerts (eds.) (2000). *Lead Mining in the Peak District*. Landmark Publishing.

Greenlees, Kay (2005). *Creating Sketchbooks for Embroiderers and Textile Artists*. Batsford.

Handy, Charles (1999). *Understanding Organisations*. Penguin.

Hedley, Gwen (2010). *Drawn to Stitch*. Batsford.

Kovats, Tania (ed.) (2007). *The Drawing Book*. Black Dog Publishing.

La Plantz, Shereen (1995). *Cover to Cover*. Lark Books.

Maitland, Sara (2008). *A Book of Silence*. Granta.

Manie, Ann (2012). *Mixed Messages: The Versatility of Collage*. A&C Black.

Maslen, Mick and Jack Southern (2011). *Drawing Projects: An Exploration of the Language of Drawing*. Black Dog Publishing.

Meech, Sandra (2009). *Connecting Art to Stitch*. Batsford.

Meech, Sandra (2012). *Connecting Design to Stitch*. Batsford.

Muntus, Rosemary (1988). *Sashiko: A Japanese Sewing Technique*. Rosemary and Thyme.

Oei, Loan and Cecile De Kegel (2002). *The Elements of Design*. Thames and Hudson.

Osler, Dorothy (1987). *Traditional British Quilts*. Batsford.

Osler, Dorothy (1991). *Quilting*. Merehurst.

Osler, Dorothy (2000). *North Country Quilts, Legend and Living Tradition*. Bowes Museum.

Pawson, Des (1998). *Handbook of Knots*. Dorling Kindersley.

Pesenti, Allegra (2010). *Rachel Whiteread Drawings*. Hammer Museum.

Quilters' Guild (1995) (2010). *Quilt Treasures*. Anne Macdonald Books.

Reade, Julian (1998). *Assyrian Sculpture*. British Museum.

Robinson, Tim (2008). *Connemara: The Last Pool of Darkness*. Penguin Ireland.

Picture credits

Pages 4, 7, 13, 20, 48, 74, 75, 77, 106, 107, 114, 115, 123: Dick Makin; pages 10 (right), 12, 14–18, 21 (bottom), 22, 23, 28 (left), 29, 31, 32, 34, 35, 37, 51, 64 (right), 67 (all images except top right), 73 (left), 81 (top and right), 116, 117, 118, 119 Helen Parrott; pages 94 and 125 Quilters' Guild of the British Isles; 21 (top) Victoria Nowell; 67 (top right) Malcolm Warrington. All other images by Michael Wicks.

Index

Make a mark on your next project
with these exciting resources from Interweave

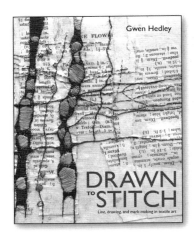

Drawn to Stitch

Line, Drawing, and Mark-Making in Textile Art

Gwen Hedley
ISBN 978-1-59668-233-7
$29.95

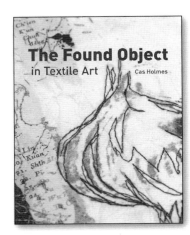

The Found Object in Textile Art

Cas Holmes
ISBN 978-1-59668-332-7
$26.95

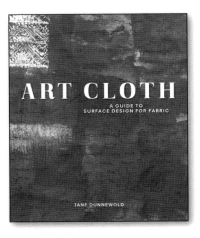

Art Cloth

A Guide to Surface Design for Fabric

Jane Dunnewold
ISBN 978-1-59668-195-8
$26.95

Available at your favorite local retailer, or

Quilting Daily Shop

shop.quiltingdaily.com

Quilting Arts MAGAZINE

Whether you consider yourself a contemporary quilter, fiber artist, art quilter, embellished quilter, or wearable art artist, *Quilting Arts Magazine* strives to meet your creative needs. **Quiltingdaily.com**

Quilting Daily

Quiltingdaily.com, the online contemporary quilting community, offers free patterns, expert tips and techniques, e-newsletters, blogs, forums, videos, special offers, and more! **Quiltingdaily.com**